The author, Mr Jimmy Wren,
and the publisher Mr Tom Breen, wish to
acknowledge the generous assistance
provided by
the management of **Arnotts** Plc.
towards the production of The Villages of Dublin.

The Villages of Dublin by Jimmy Wren   Price £4.95p

Foreword

In recent years there has been growing concern to save Dublin's historical and architectural heritage. Too often, however, that has been taken to mean the area between the city's canals. The Millennium seems a fitting time to again focus attention on Dublin's villages.

Marino's Casino, All Hallow House in Drumcondra, Malahide Castle and Clondalkin's Round Tower are some of the more prominent buildings of national importance to have survived. There have been far more lost. Frascati House, Santry Court, Old Bawn House, innumerable mediaeval castles and ecclesiastical buildings are among the casualties.

Yet the relevance of local history to the community has never been of greater importance than today. Tens of thousands of Dubliners from the 'historic' inner city are being rehoused in new satellite towns with little or no knowledge of the old communities on which they are being grafted.

Many of Dublin's villages have witnessed events which were important, not only in the history of the city, but also in the history of the nation. Every school child knows of the Battle of Clontarf, but how many people know that Dalkey was Ireland's main port for 500 years, or that Tallaght and Castleknock far exceed Wood Quay in antiquity.

No one would suggest that a knowledge of local history on its own will solve the problems of resettlement and enable the new residents of these areas to create a new identity. But local history is an important part of this process, and one of the most encouraging developments of recent years has been the revival of interest in local history.

The Old Dublin Society has played a key role in that revival. Its membership is not confined to academics but embraces a wide cross section of Dubliners, native born and 'blow-ins'. Jimmy Wren, a native of Donnycarney, has used a rare combination of skills as a historian and as an artist to put the history of Dublin's villages into a readily accessible form and he has provided in 'The Villages of Dublin' a very useful addition to the capital's retrospective in its Millennium Year.

The Rt. Hon. The Lord Mayor
Alderman Carmencita Hederman
October 1987

FRONT COVER: The launching of the Vikings. A dolmen at Howth. St. Patrick and his followers. The GPO in 1916. Dubliners Sean O'Casey, Stephen Roche and Ron Delaney.

BACK COVER: The Cullenswood massacre 1209. Olaf Cuaran. William Sarsfield. St. Brigid. Countess Markievicz. Daniel O'Connell. Dean Swift.

Cover Design by Nicholas Cloake. Layout by Margaret O'Leary. Typesetting by General Typesetting Ltd. 8 Royal Terrace West, Dun Laoghaire. Printed by Grenville Printing Co. Dublin 1.

PUBLISHED BY TOMAR PUBLISHING, BLOOM HOUSE, 78 ECCLES STREET, DUBLIN 7. TELEPHONE 302899.

The Villages of Dublin
An Introduction

"Near yonder thorn that lifts its head on high,
Where once the sign-post caught the passing eye,
Now lies that house where nut-brown draughts inspired,
Where grey-beard mirth and smiling toil retired,
Where village statesmen talked with looks profound,
And news much older than their ale went round."

Oliver Goldsmith, like Jimmy Wren, was a lover of the Irish village — "Seat of his youth where every sport could please". Goldsmith's statue outside Trinity College stands on part of the former Hoggen Green, one of Dublin's oldest villages, which in mediaeval times had its timbered cabins on the banks of the River Slayne, and within the shadows of the then timbered Dublin Castle.

Under Norman rule a ring of protective castles, fortified mansions, and tower-houses, was built along a suitable frontier, westwards and northwards of Dublin City, to ensure protection for the Pale. In the course of time dwellings, orchard-gardens, plantations, mills, taverns and forges developed within the vicinity of these castles. These clusters of human activity, busy with defence, agriculture, crafts, manufacture and industry, became villages of distinction. Sadly, many of the castles, from which they spawned, have now disappeared due to enemy attacks, or the ravages of time.

By years of diligent and scholarly research the neglected history of these outlying hamlets has been uncovered for us by Jimmy Wren in a fine wedding of text and drawings. The author of the "Deserted Village", himself a verbal landscape painter, would have approved of this present work, and its author.

Pat Johnston
Dublin Civic Museum
October 1987.

JIMMY WREN is a self-taught artist wno works in the day time as a housing supervisor with Dublin Corporation. However he has devoted most of his spare time to developing his talent as a painter and illustrator.

His other main interests are local history and gaelic sports. A former hurler with St. Laurence O'Toole's GAA club and Dublin, Jimmy has written a history of the club. He is also a member of the Old Dublin Society. A native of Donnycarney, Jimmy still lives there with his wife.

Copyright © Jimmy Wren 1987

Abbotstown and Ashtown

Little Ashtown was originally part of the lands of the priory of St. John the Baptist in Dublin. On the dissolution of the monasteries by Henry VIII Little Ashtown was granted to a Richard Netterville.

Another family to acquire lands locally was the Connels of Pelletstown, where several mills were located in the early 17th century. In 1663 some 15 acres of the Connells' lands were purchased for The Phoenix Park. A house known as 'The Phoenix House' had stood in the grounds since 1618 and had been the vice regal lodge of Cromwell's son Henry, when the latter was Lord Deputy of Ireland in the 1650s. Like Ashtown the property had originally belonged to the church, in this case the Hospitallers of Kilmainham.

After the restoration of the Stuarts, on Cromwell's death, James Butler, the First Duke of Ormonde, became Viceroy. He promptly set to work with his Chancellor, Sir Maurice Eustace, on creating a royal deer park on the site. It cost over £60,000, an astronomic sum in the 17th century, and was originally 2,000 acres in extent. It was reduced to 1,750 acres in 1680, the same size as today, and is the largest enclosed park in Europe.

The Park derives its name from a spring of clear water, Fionn Uisge. It was enclosed by Ormonde primarily to protect it from inroads of ruthless speculators, which has helped its survival to the present day. This did not prevent poachers destroying the stock of game birds specially imported for The Park by Ormonde and the original stock of deer were also poached or rustled.

The Park houses many establishments, including the American ambassador's residence, the Garda headquarters (formerly a military baracks) and the Ordnance Survey. But by far the most distinguished building is the Vice Regal Lodge, now Aras An Uachtaran, the home of the President. It was original-ly a mid-18th century Ranger's house but was enlarged and transformed by Francis Johnston, a contemporary of Gandon. Johnston also designed the GPO in O'Connell Street.

The most notorious incident connected with The Park was the murder of Lord Frederick Cavendish, the new Chief Secretary, and his Under Secretary, Thomas Burke by The Invincibles on May 6th, 1882. The Invincibles were a splinter physical force group whose action threatened for a time the land reform campaign of Parnell and Michael Davitt.

The last of the Connels, Maurice, lost his lands in 1688 when the Stuarts were deposed by the British parliament and William of Orange ascended the throne as William III. Ashtown Castle, the home of the Connels, became the Under Secretary's lodge.

Abbotstown was originally part of the barony of Castleknock. In the early 18th century Abbotstown House became the home of Richard Clements, grandfather of the First Earl of Leitrim. Shortly afterwards Admiral Sir William Rowley appears as a tenant and it was then acquired by the Falkiners, a leading family of Dublin bankers. Frederick James Falkiner was a member of the Irish House of Commons for County Dublin when the Act of Union was passed. No promise of an honour or bribe could persuade him to support the measure. He was later awarded the freedom of the city by his fellow citizens for his services to the nation, but died in poor circumstances in Naples in 1824.

A contemporary of Frederick Falkiner was Lord Holmpatrick, who built Sheephill House near Abbotstown and the new local authority housing estate there takes its name from it. The house was de-molished some years ago. Holmpatrick's family name was Hamilton and successive members of the family represented the local borough as conservative MPs in 13 parliaments, initially opposing and then staunchly defending the Act of Union.

In 1782 Dunsink was chosen as a site for the observatory by the University of Dublin under the trusts of the will of Provost Andrews. A number of distinguished figures have been associated with it, including Sir William Hamilton and Sir Robert Ball. In 1829 the poet, William Wordsworth, was a guest of Sir William Hamilton at the observatory and afterwards Sir William wrote a poem in honour of the occasion:

When beneath my roof a guest he came
And wandered with me through
pleasant walks
That, all around, make rich my home
beloved.

In more turbulent times in the early part of this century Ashtown became the scene of one of the most famous incidents of the War of Independence, when members of the Second Dublin Battalion of the Irish Volunteers ambushed the Lord Lieutenant, Field Marshal Lord French, with the assistance of the legendary Dan Breen and Sean Treacy. The incident took place at the Ashtown gate to The Park as Lord French was driven under heavy escort from the local railway station to the Viceregal Lodge. The ambush party met in The Half-Way House on December 19th, 1919.

Lord French escaped but in the bitter fight that followed one of the volunteers, Lieutenant Martin Savage of the Second Battalion, who had only joined the ambush party by chance the night before, was killed.

ASHTOWN & PHOENIX PARK

THE FAMOUS AMBUSH ATTEMPT ON LORD FRENCH TOOK PLACE AT ASHTOWN CROSS IN DECEMBER 1919. AMONG THE I.R.A. PARTY LED BY DAN BREEN WAS MARTIN SAVAGE WHO DIED FROM A THROAT WOUND THERE.

THE PHOENIX PARK RACECOURSE AT ASHTOWN WAS FOUNDED IN 1902. ORIGINALLY A STEEPLE CHASING COURSE, IT IS NOW SOLELY USED FOR FLAT RACING.

DURING THE 18TH AND EARLY 19TH CENTURIES MANY DUELS TOOK PLACE ON WHAT IS NOW THE 15 ACRES OF THE PHOENIX PARK

IN 1745 LORD CHESTERFIELD OPENED UP THE PHOENIX PARK TO THE PUBLIC. HE WAS RESPONSIBLE FOR THE ERECTION OF THE PHOENIX MONUMENT (ABOVE)

J WREN

Artane

Ara Tain

(Height of the Flocks)

The redbricked hamlet of Artane on the Malahide Road dates from the late Victorian period, when agricultural workers' cottages were built there to replace a number of thatched cabins. The meaning of the ancient denomination of Artane is now somewhat uncertain for, from three different sources, we have the following interpretations - Ard Tain meaning the Height of the Flocks, Ard Aidhean or Aidhean's Height, and Ard Ín or the Little Height.

The lands of Artane were acquired by Robert De Hollywood, Chief Remembrancer of the Exchequer, or Crown debt collector in the 14th century. This Anglo-Norman family held property in the counties of Dublin, Meath, and Wexford. The townland of Hollywood near the Naul was also in their possession.

The great European scholar and mathematician John De Hollywood was a member of this family. He was educated at Oxford and later went to Paris, where he wrote several learned works. John De Hollywood died in Paris about 1235 and was buried there in the Convent of Saint Maturine.

During the dark days of religious persecution and plantation, for 23 years between 1603 and 1626, the courageous Father Christopher Hollywood presided over the Jesuit mission in Ireland. Christopher Hollywood, son of Nicholas Hollywood Lord of the manor of Artane and Great Hollywood, was born in his father's castle at Artane in 1559.

Having studied at the University of Padua he entered the Society of Jesus at Dole, France, in 1584 and, while on a mission to Ireland, he was arrested and imprisoned in the Tower of London. Father Hollywood suffered great hardships in prison and was released after the death of Elizabeth in 1603, when he returned to his native land.

He returned to a land where he was hunted and pursued on many occasions but he always managed to elude his pursuers. One of his favourite hiding places was Dunsoghley Castle near St. Margaret's, the home of his kinsman Sir Christopher Plunkett. Father Hollywood died on the 4th September 1626 and Southwell wrote of him, "he governed the Irish million for 23 years with so much prudence, charity, zeal and fortitude in the most difficult times while persecution raged against catholics".

On the 28th July 1534 John Allen, the Archbishop of Dublin, was dragged from the castle of Artane and barbarously murdered before its great door by the followers of Silken Thomas Fitzgerald. Thomas Fitzgerald, Lord Offaly, who was then scarcely 21 years of age and was called Silken Thomas because of his flamboyant mode of apparel, had risen in rebellion against the Crown. When false rumours had been circulated by Allen and others that the Earl of Kildare, the father of Silken Thomas, had been executed in London the young Geraldine rushed to St. Mary's Abbey and flung down the Sword of State.

Archbishop Allen, an enemy of the House of Kildare, fearful of Silken Thomas' revenge, made an attempt to flee the country in great haste. The light barque in which he sailed was however, driven on shore by a storm and, after landing at Clontarf, he sought refuge at Artane Castle with his friend Thomas St. Lawrence, the guardian of the young lord of that manor. He was discovered there by the Geraldines and, when brought before the rebel leader Silken Thomas, was reported to have issued the command "take away with the clown", which was mistaken for his squires Nicholas Weafer and squires Nicholas Weafer and John Teeling for "make away with the clown" when they set upon the unfortunate churchmen and butchered him.

During the rebellion of 1641 the little Fingallian army under the command of Luke Netterville, of Corballis, garrisoned Artane Castle. After a raid for arms on two vessels in the Pool of Clontarf a party of soldiers led by Sir Charles Coote, Commander of the Garrison of Dublin, burned a considerable portion of that town. Netterville and his men then left Artane and made a stand against the military in a glen about a mile to the south of Swords, which has since been known as Bloody Hollow.

In 1825 Matthew Boyle, a wealthy Mary St. linen merchant, raised the ancient Seat of the Hollywoods at Artane and erected a modern residence in the grounds which he also called Artane Castle. The first school, established under the Industrial Schools' Act, was set up by the Christian Brothers at Artane in 1870. The school, with its fine range of workshops and buildings, was developed under the managership of the first superior Rev. Brother Thomas Hoope. With accommodation for 800 boys Artane Industrial School, which was once considered the most remarkable of its kind in Europe, closed in 1969.

ARTANE

IN 1825 WHEN THE ANCIENT CASTLE OF THE HOLLYWOOD FAMILY WAS DEMOLISHED AT ARTANE A PRIVATE RESIDENCE WAS ERECTED IN THE GROUNDS AND WAS ALSO CALLED ARTANE CASTLE (RIGHT).

THE FIRST SCHOOL UNDER THE INDUSTRIAL SCHOOLS ACT WAS ESTABLISHED BY THE IRISH CHRISTIAN BROS. AT ARTANE IN 1870. THE SCHOOL WHICH WAS THE MOST REMARKABLE OF ITS KIND IN EUROPE WAS CLOSED IN 1969.

IN 1534 ARTANE CASTLE WAS THE SCENE OF THE MURDER OF JOHN ALLEN, ARCHBISHOP OF DUBLIN BY THE FOLLOWERS OF SILKEN THOMAS.

Balbriggan

Like many placenames in Ireland the north county Dublin name of Balbriggan has several alleged sources. The name preferred locally is Baile Bricin (the town of the small trout) but Baile Brigin (the town of the small hills) is another possibility, or Baile Brecan (the town of Brecan — a Celtic saint who was abbot of Moville in Donegal and Bishop of Ard Brecan, Co Meath).

Lying 20 miles north of Dublin city, Balbriggan was totally dependent on fishing until the mid-18th century. It's earliest recorded event of significance was the baptism by St. Patrick of his successor, St. Begnignus in the river Delvin that flows through the area.

In 1329, when John Bermingham, Earl of Louth was elevated to the palatinate of that county a bitter quarrel ensued with leading anglo-norman families opposed to the appointment. This resulted in a bloody battle at Balbriggan on Whitsun Eve, when 60 followers of the Verdors, Gernons and Savages were slain.

From the earliest times the sound and sight of marching armies were familiar to the villagers of Balbriggan. Through it came the victorious but mournful Dalcassians, bearing King Brian after Clontarf and in 1649 Oliver Cromwell passed through en route for Drogheda. On July 3rd, 1690, William of Orange set up camp at Balbriggan after his victory at the Boyne.

Not surprisingly, there were a mere 30 or so inhabitants by the late 17th century and the population stagnated until 1780 when a philanthropic local landlord, Baron Hamilton, introduced cotton manufacturing and laid the basis for expansion.

George Baron Hamilton was the son of Alexander Hamilton, a Co. Down man who bought the estates of Balbriggan and Balrothery from the Barnewell family in 1718. The Barnewells had owned them for centuries. His son George was to become MP for Belfast, Solicitor General and Baron of the Exchequer in recognition of his efforts to promote Irish trade and commerce. his cotton and hosiery factory at Balbriggan was founded with a government grant of £1,230 and created employment for two centuries in the town.

The hosiery goods of Smyth and Company were known worldwide and their brandname of "Balbriggans" was familiar in the United States as a synonym for Long Johns. Smyco made silk stockings for Queen Victoria on a special loom in the factory. In 1896 the company employed 600 people and kept two schools of embroidery, one at Skerries and the other at Rush, employing 40 girls in each. The goods of the Balbriggan factory won many prizes at international trade exhibitions, including the gold medal at the Great Chicago Exhibition of

1893. In April 1980 Smyth and Company went into liquidation. It was the second oldest public firm in Ireland (the oldest was Guinness) and the longest standing member of the Dublin stock exchange.

Just to the north of Balbriggan is the townland of Bremore (the large hill). It has five tumuli, believed to contain passage graves. The townland also contains the wall of an ancient church called Lambeecher, with which two celtic saints, Molagga and Modhomnoc were connected. The chapelry of Lambeecher (the beekeepers church from Llan - welsh for church, Beech - bee and aire -keeper) was founded in the 7th century by the Munster saint, Molagga. He received the land on which the church was built as a gift, after curing the local chief of the Ciannachta sept of a serious illness when the druids had failed. Molagga is commemorated in Templemolaga, his birthplace in Co. Cork from whence he travelled to Wales to become a disciple of St. David before spreading the gospel in Ireland.

St. Modhomnoc, or Domnoc, was another Irishman associated with the Welsh patron saint, David. He helped him lay out his monastery garden at Menevia. While there he learnt to cultivate hived bees and brought the knowledge with him back to Ireland. Legend has it that a swarm of bees followed his ship back to Ireland, but other sources claim that it was Molagga who acquired some of Domnoc's swarm and introduced the superior bee culture to north county Dublin.

On the southern outskirts of Balbriggan lies Balrothery which, in mediaeval times, was an important centre of the Norman administration in the Pale. Council and parliaments were frequently held there, hence its name (town of the riders or knights). The protestant church at Balrothery has incorporated in it the square mediaeval tower with a celtic round tower at one angle of the building overlooking the present day village and main Dublin–Belfast road.

In 1318 the local magnate, Sir Hugh de Lacy, was dispossessed of his lands because he sided with the Scots invader, Edward Bruce. in the 16th century Balrothery was described as "amongst the good and walled towns of this County" and in 1641 three annual fairs and a

weekly market were still being held there, despite the warlike times.

The Lord Deputy, Sir Henry Sidney, visited the castle and his master of horse, Christopher Wren, made the following entry in his account book for January 1577. "Horses bought at Bullrotherye for six shillings. My Lord lying there, riding toward north parts".

Early in the last century many robbers and highwaymen plied their trade on the north coach road around Balbriggan. On September 21st, 1810, Captain Grierson a magistrate from the town, with a party of Yeomanry, arrested two Loughlins who were noted robbers, one of them had a clubbed foot. Also captured were Flynn of the Naul and Kennedy a blacksmith, as well as a fiddler who harboured them. Grierson was credited with ridding the area of freebooters.

In Balrothery churchyard a palin headstone stands over the grave of eight sailors who lost their lives, along with seven other crew members, in a tempest off this coastline in 1875. The Bella Hill, a large three masted vessel, had left Liverpool for Valparaiso with a crew of 16 hands under Captain Edgar and a general cargo on board. On February 26th the vessel was driven onto the reefs nearby at Newhaven and Bremore and broke up. Heroic efforts by local people and coastguards failed to save all but one of the crew, James McDonnell, who refused to comment on local rumours that a mutiny was the cause of the mishap. In 1873 a Wicklow bound collier, the "Sarah of Runcorn" was lost with four hands while the Skerries lifeboat, which went to its aid, capsized losing six crewmen.

During the famine, in January 1847, a bread cart was stopped and attacked at Balbriggan by a number of starving men. The men, who were employed by the Board of Works on relief work had not been paid their wages - due to the illness of the wages clerk. A local curate, Fr. Grimley, persuaded them to allow the cart to proceed and they were later paid at the residence of the local surveyor for the Board.

Harry Reynolds, one of Ireland's greatest cyclists, came from Balbriggan. He began his career in 1892 and, in August 1896, he won the world amateur

(Continued on Page 74)

BALBRIGGAN

ABOUT A HALF MILE NORTH OF BALBRIGGAN IS THE TOWNLAND OF BREMORE WHERE THE 7TH CENTURY SAINT MOLAGGA FOUNDED A CHURCH. WHEN HE CURED A LOCAL CIANNACHTA CHIEF OF DISEASE AFTER THE DRUIDS HAD FAILED TO DO SO HE WAS GIVEN THE LANDS OF BREMORE AS A GIFT

ON JULY THE 3RD 1690 WILLIAM OF ORANGE AND HIS ARMY ENCAMPED AT BALBRIGGAN AFTER THE BATTLE OF THE BOYNE.

ON SEPT. 20TH 1920 A BLACK AND TAN FORCE IN REPRISAL FOR THE SHOOTING OF AN R.I.C. OFFICER SACKED AND BURNED THE TOWN OF BALBRIGGAN

HARRY REYNOLDS "THE BALBRIGGAN FLYER" WON THE AMATEUR MILE CYCLING CHAMPIONSHIP OF THE WORLD AT COPENHAGEN IN 1896.

JWREN

Baldoyle

Baile Dubh Gall   (Town of the Dark Strangers)

The name Baldoyle dates from the 9th century when Scandinavian pirates established a stronghold or base here. They used it to plunder the treasure-rich monasteries of Leinster. For almost 200 years, until their crushing defeat at Clontarf in 1014, viking longships laden with booty and slaves sailed into this sheltered creek to the north of the isthmus of the Howth peninsular.

These Danish vikings who settled here were known by the native Irish as dubh gall, or dark strangers, hence the name Baile Dubh Gall, or Town of the Dark Strangers.

In 1012 the territory of the Northmen in Fingal was attacked by King Malachy and his Meathmen, which resulted in the razing of the Baldoyle fortress.

At Howth Malachy defeated a Norse force as well, but on his return to the Royal County he was surprised at Drynam near Swords. The vikings were led by Sitric, king of Dublin, and he defeated Malachy's army slaying his son Flann and many others.

Up until the Anglo-Norman invasion a portion of the Baldoyle lands remained in the possession of a Danish chieftain. Hamund McTorkaill was the last of these, losing his lands like other north county Dublin landholders to the new invaders.

About 1150 Dermot McMurrough, king of Leinster and ally of the Anglo-Normans, founded the Priory of All Hallows on the present site of Trinity College, Dublin. So the process of absorbing the Norse city and its environs into Leinster predates the Anglo-Norman invasion.

The significance of Dermot's new foundation for Baldoyle was that some years later the lands of Baldoyle were presented to the new priory. With the endowment went a family headed by Melisu Mac Feilican, and his sons and grandsons.

Baldoyle became the grange, or home farm, for the monks. A parish chapel was built here, probably late in the 13th century, for the tenants, villeins and serfs of the grange.

In 1369 a meeting was held in this little church, known as the hungry parliament. The Lord Lieutenant of the day, Sir William de Windsor, assembled together a large gathering of Anglo-Norman magnates whom he had deprived of food and lodging and compelled to vote in favour of levying subsidies for the crown. As the church only measured 18 feet by 45 feet the feudal lords must have had to endure severe overcrowding along with their other privations.

By the 16th century the possessions of the Priory of All Hallows at Baldoyle included 20 gardens, 60 acres of arable land, four acres of meadow, 16 acres of pasture, one acre of copse and a warren on another acre. There were also four messauges (dwelling houses and outbuildings with land assigned), five cottages, 200 acres of arable land, 12 acres of meadow, 12 acres of pasture and four acres of wood in the grange of Baldoyle.

The monks of All Hallows worked the Baldoyle grange farm until 1536, when Henry VIII suppressed the monastery and confiscated its lands, granting them to the corporation of Dublin.

In 1615 Patrick Beahan was incumbent at Baldoyle and, by 1630, it was reported that the grange church was in ruins with nothing but the bare walls standing. This ancient ruin, locally referred to as Grange Abbey, still stands today in a field near Donaghmeade shopping centre surrounded by modern housing estates.

The building had stout walls two-and-a-half feet thick. There is evidence of a timber roof in holes that were made in the gables. The east and west windows were originally decorated with sharply cut tracery of which nothing remains today.

Outside the ruined church are some cypress trees and beneath their branches are two 18th century headstones with finely cut inscriptions. One is the burial stone of James Quinn of Coolock and his family, dated 1736, while the other commemorates John Dundas, who died in 1737. These memorials indicate that burials were made here long after the church itself fell into ruins.

This little ruined church is a historic link with the mediaeval past in south-east Fingal and, a few years ago, a praiseworthy effort to clean it up was made by the Donaghmeade residents association. At present this ancient monument and the area adjacent to it is in a neglected and untidy state and is in urgent need of attention from the local authorities or the office of public works, which is charged with protecting our national heritage.

Baldoyle has had an inn or hostelry of some kind since at least the early 17th century, as witnessed by one of the oldest Irish hunting songs in existence, preserved amongst the Sloan manuscripts in the British Museum. It concerns Michael St. Lawrence of the Howth family and a group of his friends who, after a day's hunting went to the town of Baldoyle for refreshments.

> *"The drink it was good and so was the bread,*
> *They took of their liquor till they were all red,*
> *And when they had done they sang the hare's knell,*
> *And if I had more, faith the more I would tell".*

When the corporation of Dublin came into possession of Baldoyle they granted the grange to Sir Edward FitzSimons and, in 1659, the census recorded that only 26 people lived there. All of them were Irish.

The Baldoyle of the eighteenth century saw a frequent visitor in the person of Dean Swift, who had several friends residing in the district. On fair summer days he rode out from the city along the large strand which then stretched from Amiens Street, through Fairview and along the seafront to Baldoyle Road.

In his letter Swift refers to his visit to Grange House, the home of Mrs. Acheson, and to a nearby house where he stayed with the Rev. Samuel Webber, the Vicar of Howth.

When Archibald Hamilton Rowan, the United Irishman, escaped from Newgate prison in 1792 he was sheltered and aided by his friend John Sweetman of Sutton. With Sweetman's help he was spirited away to France in a wherry which was manned by three Baldoyle fishermen, the two Sheridan brothers and a friend named Murphy.

(Continued on Page 40)

BALDOYLE

TOWN OF THE DARK STRANGERS

DURING THE VIKING PERIOD BALDOYLE WAS ONE OF THE DANISH STRONGHOLDS ON THE NORTH DUBLIN COAST. BALDOYLE, THE TOWN OF DUBHGALL OR DOYLE A PERSONAL NAME - - SIGNIFYING BLACKGALL OR FOREIGNER

ARCHIBALD HAMILTON ROWAN A UNITED IRISHMAN ON THE RUN WHO WITH THE AID OF THREE LOCAL FISHERMEN ESCAPED BY BOAT FROM BALDOYLE TO FRANCE IN 1792

J.WREN '78

IN 1369 A MEETING OF PARLIMENT WAS HELD IN THE SMALL CHAPEL OF THE GRANGE OF BALDOYLE UNDER VICEROY WILLIAM DE WINDSOR.

Ballybough and Clonliffe

The recently widened bridge at Ballybough (when it was named after Dublin folk singer Luke Kelly), marks the southern boundary of the ancient territory of Fingal. A bridge has spanned the Tolka at this, its lowest fording point, for over 600 years.

The first bridge was erected by the munificent mayor of Dublin, John Le Decer in 1313. Le Decer, a benefactor of religious houses and provider of the ancient water supply to the city is deserving of recognition in our street nomenclature.

Le Decer's bridge fell down during a great storm but was rebuilt and, by the 15th century, a stone bridge was standing there once more which lasted until 1938. Surprisingly there was no public outcry at its demolition.

A short distance from the bridge an old fishing weir once stood and it was here, according to several historians that Turlough, grandson of Brian, fell at the Battle of Clontarf. In celtic times the area now covered by modern day Ballybough was part of a district called Crinan which stretched between the Liffey and the Tolka and it is believed that the name Summerhill, or the Hill of Crinan, dates from this period.

The adjoining townland of Clonliffe has two interpretations. According to Joyce it means the 'plain of the herbs', while the 'plain of the Liffey' is also given. Towards the middle of the 12th century the monks of St. Mary's Abbey acquired the lands of Clonliffe, which then described an area from the sea boundary, along the present North Strand, to what is now the Phoenix Park. The Clonliffe grange lands of the Cistercians also included the grounds of the present Holy Cross College and Croke Park.

Although these lands lay within the city's boundaries they were owned by the Abbot and convent of St. Mary's, and its residents paid a tithe to St. Mary's. In 1510, when two local men, John Netterville and John Penqueyt, murdered a man and stole a sheep worth eight pence, they successfully sought sanctuary in St. Mary's. Just over 20 years later King Henry VIII dissolved the monasteries and the largest landowner in the district became John Bath of Drumcondra, who owned 80 acres.

In 1556 the Earl of Desmond leased "The Grange, fields and mill of Cloneliffe" to Matthew, King of Clontarf, in whose family interest it remained until 1619, when the title of possession was sold to Sir Garrett Moore of Melifont, Co. Louth. Sir Garrett was a friend of Hugh O'Neill and concealed Hugh O'Donnell after his escape from Dublin Castle in 1592.

In 1792 Luke Gardiner became the owner of the Grange of Clonliffe.

Gardiner, after whom Gardiner Street is named, was responsible for the development of a great part of the Georgian north city of Dublin, along with his son and grandson. His grandson Luke Gardiner was a great advocate for the abolition of the penal laws against Catholics. He died at the Battle of New Ross in 1798 fighting on the Government's side.

Ballybough itself was the scene of a battle in 1534. This followed the decision of Henry VIII to destroy the great Fitz-Gerald dynasty, which had effectively ruled Ireland for many years. When the ninth earl was imprisoned in the Tower of London his son, Silken Thomas, besieged Dublin and used Ballybough as a base in 1534.

The area was left comparatively unscathed during subsequent rebellions and, from the 1650s, many Jewish refugees from Europe settled in Ballybough from England, after Cromwell granted them asylum under his regime. In 1717 they built the first Jewish cemetery on what is now Fairview Strand, beside the village. For the rest of the century the village of Annadale on Philipsburgh Avenue was the main centre of Jewry in Ireland, containing some 40 families of 200 souls. After a new synagogue was built in the 1790s, at Marlborough Green near the Customs House, the local community dwindled rapidly.

During the eighteenth century Ballybough also became a busy manufacturing centre. Flour and oat mills were erected along the Tolka and powered by a millrace. The premises cost £100 a year to rent. Apart from the commercially vigorous Jewish community, a major contribution to the area's prosperity was Captain Philip Roche, who fought for James II at Limerick and later served in the French King's forces. While on the Continent Roche learnt how to manufacture flint glass and returned home to establish a glass works at Ballybough. During the eighteenth century glass utensils and plate glass for windows and coaches were to be amongst Ireland's few manufactured exports. Later, the factory, which stood beside the old bridge on the city side of the Tolka, the converted to a vitriol plant. Meanwhile, according to the 'Dublin Chronicle' of 1787, the village also housed iron mills which manufactured spades, shovels "and other implements of husbandry and kitchenware" previously imported from

abroad.

In 1710 one Tristram Fortick leased land and a house at Clonliffe which was marked on Rocque's map of 1756 as Fortick's Grove. The building known as the Red House on the grounds of Holy Cross College stands on the site of an earlier dwelling house which was occupied by Fortick in the early 18th century. When Fortick lived here Clonliffe Road was a narrow pathway called Fortick's Lane.

Where it met Ballybough Road at the present advertisement hoarding there was once a suicide burial plot. Here the bodies of suicides were transfixed with stakes to prevent them from rising to obtain a Christian burial. According to a newspaper report there was a belief in the area that some unhappy spirits had freed themselves and roamed the district. For many years "none but the bravest or most inebriated crossed Ballybough Bridge at the witching hour" said the reporter.

The Red House at Clonliffe was the scene of a violent affray in 1806 when a gang of robbers, led by the highwayman Larry Clinch, were surprised by a party of military as they attempted to relieve Buck Jones of his valuables. In the ensuing fight two of the robbers were killed and several others died of their wounds. The corpses were exposed for some days and when relatives proved reluctant to claim them they were buried in the suicides plot.

Buck Jones, after whom Jones's Road was named, became extremely unpopular with the majority of Dublin citizens because of his role as a magistrate in the 1798 period. Eventually he was forced to close down his theatre and died in poverty in a wretched cabin on the site of the present Mountjoy Prison. For many years after his death it was claimed that his ghost rode a white horse in the vicinity of Jones's Road after dark.

Between 1845 and 1857 the Red House (Clonliffe House) was occupied by the Department of Inland Revenue. It was then purchased by Archbishop Cullen of Dublin as a seminary for the diocese. Holy Cross seminary was opened in September 1859 and four years later, on May 19th, 1863, Archbishop Cullen performed the opening ceremonies for the present college building.

Mud Island is the name given to a

Continued on Page 14

BALLYBOUGH

THE OLD STONE BRIDGE AT BALLYBOUGH WHICH WAS REPLACED IN 1938 AND OLD VITRIOL WORKS (IN BACKGROUND) ON SITE OF PRESENT FLAT SCHEME.

MUD ISLAND BALLYBOUGH HAD IN THE LAST CENTURY A PRIZE FIGHTING TRADITION. JACK LANGAN A LOCAL HERO BATTLED ON TWO OCCASIONS WITH TOM SPRING FOR THE ENGLISH CROWN

IN 1534 SILKEN THOMAS AND HIS FOLLOWERS DEFEATED A COMPANY OF ENGLISH SOLDIERS AT BALLYBOUGH BRIDGE.

THE POET JAMES CLARENCE MANGAN WAS A REGULAR VISITOR AT THE PUBLIC HOUSE KEPT BY HIS FRIEND AND FELLOW POET LAURENCE BLIGH AT BALLYBOUGH.

settlement of mud cabins which, in the 17th and 18th centuries, lay on the city side of Ballybough Bridge. According to tradition a colony was founded there by three McDonnell brothers dispossessed during the Ulster plantation of 1606. Mud Island became a notorious haunt for smugglers and highwaymen who elected their own 'king', usually from the McDonnell clan. When Mud Island King Art Granger died under a hail of excise bullets in 1759 his ghost was said to have joined the already crowded spirit population of the area. Another Mud Island monarch, Grid Iron McDonnell, on one occasion escaped from the Sheriff and a regiment of soldiers dressed as a woman and after being arrested in 1820 was rescued by a party of coal porters.

In former times Mud Island was renowned for its prize fighting tradition and many a battle took place there in what was known as the big meadow. Jack Langan was the most famous Mud Island pugilist and his fight with Norman, also from the island, is reputed to have lasted several hours. After his 35 round defeat of McGowan at the Curragh in 1819, Langan pursued his pugilistic career across the Irish Sea. There he fought Tom spring unsuccessfully for the championship of England on two occasions. After his retirement he was a pub landlord in Liverpool for a number of years and a well known supporter of Daniel O'Connell. When he died, in March 1846, the 'Freeman's Journal' described him as "the possessor of an undying affection for his native land".

In the 18th and 19th centuries Ballybough public houses were famous for their Dublin Bay oysters and cockles. James O'Keeffe, the Dublin actor, refers in his memoirs to visits with theatrical friends to Hallogan's tavern in Ballybough, which was known as The Cockle Hall. In 1787, when James Brunton was

its proprietor, an English writer R. Lewis, referred to it "as suited for accommodation of Dublin citizens, lovers of oysters and stewed cockles". It was frequented by such personalities as pugilists Jack Langan and his trainer, the famous Dan Donnelly, Collier the robber, Bryan 'Bully' Maguire the duellist, Davy Ball and Watty Cox of 'Irish Magazine' notoriety.

The present 'Fairview Inn' on Fairview Strand dates from the 18th century, when it was known as Paddy Ready Penny's Ale House. The owner of the time, Paddy Reigh, was a shrewd businessman who held the view that credit was a shortlived customer and laid the foundation for a successful business that remained in his family for several generations.

That unhappy genius James Clarence Mangan was a frequent visitor to the public house on Ballybough Road kept by his fellow poet and friend, Laurence Bligh. Here, in the early 1820s, the young Mangan spent many evenings in the convivial company of Bligh, James Tighe and other writers. In after years we are told that "while seated in Bligh's cozy bar parlour overlooking that deserted swamp, the North Lotts, some of Mangan's sarcastical compositions were thrown off, apparently without an effort". The deserted North Lotts referred to were that part of the East Wall reclaimed from the sea during the 18th century. Laurence Bligh was a native of Kilmurry, Co. Meath, and his pub at 23 Ballybough Road stood between the present Annesley Garage and O'Sullivan Avenue. The 'Fluther Good' public house at Ballybough is named after a local character of that name who has been immortalised in Sean O'Casey's play, 'The Plough and the Stars'.

During the 1916 period there was much republican activity in the Bally-

bough and Fairview areas. Fr. Matthew Park, which was situated at the rere of the Fairview R.C. church was a Dublin Brigade parade ground, where many of the guns from the 1914 gunrunning operation at Howth were stored. The Clann na hEireann Hall at Richmond Road, opposite Ballybough Bridge, was a Sinn Fein and Gaelic League centre frequented by Eamon Ceannt, Sean O'Casey, Sean Connolly, Peadar Kearney and many others involved in Irish cultural as well as military activities of the time.

On Easter Monday 1916 over 100 volunteers under the command of Captain Thomas Weafer came under fire from troops on the Northern Railway line and defensive positions were set up between the Royal Canal bridge and Annesley Bridge. The main body of the rebels were later ordered to the GPO but a party under the command of Sean Russell held out near the Annesley Bridge until Wednesday evening, when they were ordered to withdraw. A monument to Russell, who later became chief of staff of the IRA, was erected in Fairview Park in the 1950s.

The best known feature of Ballybough today is Croke Park, which was acquired for its headquarters in 1911 by the Gaelic Athletic Association. It was bought on their behalf by Frank Dineen, a prominent member of the time. Previously to this gaelic games had been played there for 20 years, but the ground had also been used by other sporting groups. In the 1890s the owner, Maurice Butterly, JP, rented the ground as the city and suburban racecourse. It was also used for soccer and cycling. When the first annual Gaelic League carnival was held there in 1910 it was a brilliant success and the League's president, later president of Ireland, Dr. Douglas Hyde addressed the huge gathering.

CLONLIFFE

THE MAGNIFICENT CROKE PARK H.Q. OF THE G.A.A. WAS BOUGHT IN 1908 BY FRANK B. DINEEN A FORMER SEC. AND PRES. OF THE ASSOCIATION. PRIOR TO THAT IT WAS THE CITY AND SURBURBAN RACECOURSE.

DURING PÁDRAIG O CAOIMH'S TERM AS SECRETARY (1929-1964) THE CUSACK (1937) AND NEW HOGAN (1959) STANDS WERE ERECTED AND SPECTATOR ACCOMODATION INCREASED FROM 30,000 TO OVER 90,000.

ANCIENT CLONLIFFE WAS FARMED FOR CENTURIES BY THE WHITE MONKS OF SAINT MARY'S ABBEY. WHEN HOLY CROSS MISSIONARY COLLEGE WAS ESTABLISHED HERE IN 1858, THE RED HOUSE THE FORMER RESIDENCE OF FREDERICK "BUCK" JONES WAS THE FIRST SEMINARY BUILDING.

J.WREN

Ballyfermot

Baile Diarmuid (Dermot's Town)

The vast Dublin suburb of Ballyfermot derives its name from an obscure celtic chieftain, or farmer, about whom nothing certain is known.

In ancient times the tract of land overlooking the Liffey on the south side of Chapelizod was known as Baile Diarmuid, or Dermot's Town. In the course of time Baile Diarmuid became Baile Thormod, and later still Baile Formod or Ballyfermot as we know it today.

At the time of the Anglo-Norman invasion the Irish chieftain Mac Gillamocholog, son-in-law of Dermot McMurrough the King of Leinster, held the lands of Ballyfermot along with a large part of Dublin county north and south of the Liffey. Mac Gillamocholmog, who threw in his lot with the Anglo-Normans, was rewarded with land grants. These included one at Greystones, Co. Wicklow, where he and his descendants had their principal residence.

Some time before 1307 William FitzWilliam and his wife Avicia were in possession of Ballyfermot, and in that year they assigned a third of the manor to Thomas Cantock, Bishop of Emly and Chancellor of Ireland.

The remainder of the manor of Ballyfermot later passed from the FitzWilliams to their relatives, the Clahulls of Dundrum. From them it passed through marriage to the Barnawalls of Drimnagh Castle.

The Knights Hospitallers of St. John of Jerusalem, whose priory was at Kilmainham, became owners of the church at Ballyfermot in the 13th century. The church was situated near Le Fanu Road but there is no trace of it today.

Francis Elington Ball, in his history of county Dublin states: "That the structure was of late date with possibly more than one predecessor on its site". It remained in the possession of the Knights of Kilmainham until the dissolution of that house in the 16th century.

After the reformation the building at Ballyfermot was taken over and occupied by the established church, until its closure about 1660.

Austin Cooper, visiting Ballyfermot in 1781 mentions "an old church here covered in ivy and in it an old baptisimal font, but no ancient tombs". A drawing of the church is reproduced in Ball's "History of County Dublin" The building, dedicated to St. Lawrence and measuring 54 feet by 19 feet, was shown as a fairly large, roofless structure containing no features of architectural interest.

Burials were continued in the adjoining graveyard after the church's closure and ressurectionists were busy there in the early part of the last century supplying medical schools as far afield as Edinburgh and Glasgow with bodies.

A Norman type castle once stood in Ballyfermot and, when Austin Cooper saw it in 1781, he described it as a small building kept in good repair and inhabited. During Elizabethan times Ballyfermot Castle was occupied by Luke Dillon, a prominent lawyer and later Chief Baron of the Exchequer in Ireland.

Towards the end of the 16th century an Englishman named Robert Newcomen came to live in Ballyfermot. Having advanced himself in the service of Lord Mountjoy, the Lord Deputy, he was knighted in 1605. He was the ancestor of Lord Newcomen of Killester, who voted for the Act of Union in 1800 and shot himself when his Bank on Cork Hill failed in 1825.

If Sir Robert Newcomen distinguished himself in service to the crown, suppressing the great rebellion of Hugh O'Neill and Hugh Roe O'Donnell, his son Beverly, who succeeded him at Ballyfermot, had the happier distinction of ridding Irish waters of the pirates as commander of the ships guarding the coasts.

In recognition of his efforts he was knighted and appointed Admiral of Ireland, but in 1637 he met an untimely death by drowning while engaged in sounding Waterford harbour.

Sir Beverly's daughter succeeded him at Ballyfermot and she married Sir Hubert Adrian, who was Mayor of Dublin in 1660 and assumed the name of Vereer for some unknown reason.

In 1664 Sir Hubert Adrian Vereer paid hearth tax for ten hearths at Ballyfermot Castle and there were also 20 small houses here with a population of about 90 people.

Towards the end of the 18th century Austin Cooper reports a school house was built adjoining Ballyfermot Castle by William Oulton Prosser, who taught 20 pupils there. In 1781 Cooper also reported that a high mound with a large tree growing on top of it near the Castle had been partially dug away. One wonders how many such tumuli in the Dublin area have thus disappeared without archaeological excavation.

Ballyfermot also had links with the northside of Dublin through the Burnell family. In the 14th century a portion of the Ballyfermot lands belonged to Robert Burnell, whose descendants later settled in Balgriffin and were attainted by the crown when John Burnell was executed for his part in the rebellion of Silken Thomas during the reign of Henry VIII. The Burnell lands at Ballyfermot were then granted to Alderman Thady Duffe, whose family remained in occupation for several generations.

BALLYFERMOT

THE CHURCH OF SAINT LAWRENCE AT BALLYFERMOT WAS BUILT IN THE LATE 14TH CENTURY BY WOLFRAN DE BARNWELL AND LATER CAME INTO THE POSSESSION OF THE KNIGHTS HOSPITALLERS.

IN THE EARLY PART OF THE 19TH CENTURY THE LONELY GRAVEYARD OF BALLYFERMOT WAS FREQUENTLY VISITED BY RESURRECTIONISTS

J. WREN '79

IN HIS MASTERPIECE OF THE SUPERNATURAL "THE HOUSE BY THE CHURCHYARD", JOSEPH SHERIDAN LE FANU USED A BALLYFERMOT SETTING FOR THE TILED HOUSE WHICH WAS HAUNTED BY A HAND.

Ballymun

Baile Mhuinn

(Town of the Shrubland)

Before 1965, when building commenced on the new satellite town, Ballymun was flat green countryside, a portion of which was used by the Albert Agricultural College. (The College subsequently transferred to Celbridge).

The Rev. Benjamin Adams in his "History of Santry Parish" refers to Ballymun as derived from the family name of Munn (Munn's Town), but a more likely meaning is Baile Muin or "The Town of the Shrubland", a reference to the dense forest which originally grew there.

In the 14th century the Moreward family, the Barons of Scryne in Co. Meath, held the lands of Ballymun. In 1473 Richard Stanyhurst, a citizen of Dublin was granted 180 acres after his marriage to Agneta, a daughter of the Baron of Scryne.

The Burnell family of Balgriffin was also in possession of land at Ballymun for some centuries, but lost it to the Bathes of Drumcondra after John Burnell was executed for treason for supporting Silken Thomas in his insurrection of 1534.

In 1615 Robert Barnwell of Dunbro was in possession of Ballymun and a period of decline appears to have set in. By 1641 all that stood in the townland was a thatched house with two or three cottages. By 1659 the population of Ballymun was four people of English birth and six of Irish birth. Five years later the hearth tax rolls record John Browne, William Dodd, Walter Ellis and Richard Foekes as paying tax for one hearth each - a far cry from today's densely populated estate.

The Tower House at Ballymun was originally built as a mill at the beginning of the 18th century. In 1744 it was taken over by "the incorporated society of promoting English schools in Ireland".

Known as the Charter Schools, after their foundation by a Royal Charter of February 6th 1733 of George II, a number of these establishments were opened around the country to instruct the children of the catholic poor in the protestant religion.

The Ballymun establishment initially opened as a girls school. Besides being educated the girls were employed in winding silk and spinning cotton. The school was later converted to educating boys until its abolition in 1825.

The Tower House, which is now a private residence, was used as a meeting place during the Civil War. Talks were held here for the purpose of arranging a ceasefire.

Ballymun in the early 18th century was a place to be avoided by night or, for that matter during the day, as it was well wooded and afforded cover for the many highwaymen who operated along the Drogheda Road. Ballymun was also a noted place for the fighting of duels and the "Freeman's Journal" of December 9th 1829 reported one such incident which took place between Counsellor McCartney of Lower Mount Street and a Surgeon L''... McCartney was badly wounded near the groin and carried to Mr. Coughlan's (a publican) house at Santry.

The Stormanstown area of Ballymun takes its name from a Lord Stormingston who was granted land here during the reign of Henry VIII. The original Stormanstown House was erected early in the 17th century.

Described as a noble tiled mansion containing numerous apartments, it was demolished in 1823 and its materials were used in the building of another house of the same name which was situated near the present Sillogue gardens.

The house was used during this century by the Albert Agricultural College as offices and was taken down about 1970. Another house, also called Stormanstown, was erected here early in the last century and stood where the ESB offices and showrooms are now located at the corner of Ballymun Avenue and Ballymun Road.

Brian O'Higgins, the poet, scholar and Sinn Féin TD lived in this house during the Troubles and many a man on the run was sheltered here. It was also demolished in the early 1970s.

The old catholic chapel at Ballymun was erected in the year 1847 during the famine times, which was a remarkable achievement. It replaced an old penal chapel which stood near the junction of the Saint Margaret's Road and Boot Inn Road.

Behind the church is a vault enclosed in railings which was erected by the Domville family of Santry Court in memory of James Kelly, who was in their employ as a coachman. This unfortunate man perished in a most appalling manner as the victim of local whiskey-crazed bucks who poured whiskey over him and set him ablaze.

In the last century a number of 17th century French and English coins were dug up in the townland of Balcurris, where the camp of James II was located in 1690 before the army marched to the battle of the Boyne. The townland of Balcurris (Town of the Weir) derives its name from a marshland which was drained about 1845. In 1659 the population of Balcurris consisted of 13 Irish born persons and, in 1664 Peter Fox, Thady Lawless and John Welsh paid tax for one hearth each.

Poppintree is called after an ancient tree beneath which a pattern (a corruption of the word patron) was held annually on the last day of July to commemorate Saint Pappin of Santry. In the days before the Famine the local people assembled here on St. Pappin's feast day.

Poppintree House, on the back road to St. Margarets, was the home of the Carton family for generations. It is now the property of O'Shea and Shanahan, the builders. A great portion of the original Poppintree land is today covered by a modern housing estate of the same name, which was completed in 1976.

The high rise flats which marked the state of the satellite town of Ballymun were opened in 1969 by Neil Blaney, the then minister for local government. It took four years to complete the scheme at a cost of £12 million.

After more than a decade the Ballymun project has come under severe criticism over the design and basic conception of the tower blocks. Many experts maintain that the high rise buildings are unsuitable for young families and the lack of adequate facilities is breeding serious social problems.

BALLYMUN

BEFORE HE SET OUT FOR THE BOYNE IN 1690 JAMES II AND HIS ARMY ENCAMPED IN THE TOWNLAND OF BALCURRIS WHICH NOW FORMS PART OF THE HOUSING ESTATE OF BALLYMUN, BETWEEN THE YEARS 1966 AND 1969 BALLYMUN ESTATE WAS BUILT ON THE FIELDS WHICH WERE FORMERLY PORTION OF THE ALBERT AGRICULTURAL COLLEGE

THE TOWNLAND OF POPPINTREE LYING ADJACENT TO BALLYMUN IS NAMED AFTER SAINT PAPPINS TREE WHERE A PATRON WAS HELD ANNUALLY UNTIL FAMINE TIMES

BALLYMUN WAS DURING THE EIGHTEENTH CENTURY A HAUNT FOR HIGHWAYMEN WHO USED THE SHRUBLAND THERE FOR COVER.

J. WREN '80

Blanchardstown

Over the past decade hundreds of Dublin families have settled in new homes in the district of Blanchardstown and this placename dates from the 13th century, when the family of Blanchard occupied the lands here.

The Blanchards apparently came to Ireland with the Norman invasion and were connected with the Tyrrels, Lords of Castleknock and Tipperary. In the thirteenth century much of Blanchardstown and Clonsilla became church property in consequence of a grant from Richard Tyrell, Lord of Castleknock, to the Benedictines of Little Malvern in Worcestershire.

In the early 14th century, when John Owen became a local landowner, a great wood called Scald's Wood covered the area and it survived until the 17th century. Although situated only six miles from Dublin Castle, the remoteness and wildness of Blanchardstown in former ages is indicated by the fact that a public wolf hunt was ordered in Scald's Wood as late as 1652.

The monastic lands of Blanchardstown changed hands in the 15th century, when the English Benedictines of Little Malvern left and the Dublin Cistercians of St. Mary's Abbey became the new landlords. At the time of the Restoration in 1660 there were five people of English descent and 26 people of Irish descent living at Blanchardstown. Richard Berford, who was then the chief resident, bequeathed his brewing pan at Ratoath to the local villagers.

With the opening of the Royal Canal in the late 18th century a flour mill was built along its banks at Blanchardstown. Originally powered by a water wheel, goods were transporteed by barge from the mill well into the last century. Today, Crest Foods Limited own the Blanchardstown mill. Margarine, cooking fats and oil are packed there.

The Saint Brigid's Brass Band, in Blanchardstown, claims the distinction of being the oldest village band in Ireland. 1826 is given as the year of its foundation.

Formed originally in connection with the temperance movement, the earliest known bandrooms the old thatched "Society Rooms" was the garda station of today. A subsequent band headquarters was the local courthouse, which was blown up in 1922 – the bass drum was found near the River Tolka afterwards.

In 1843 the Saint Brigid's Brass and Reed Band, Blanchardstown, was amongst several bands from Dublin which attended the monster Repeal meeting called by O'Connell at Tara, marching to the ancient capital of Ireland and back.

Through the years, the band has played on many historical occasions in Dublin and in 1966 it led the Old IRA veterans into O'Connell Street on the 50th anniversary of the Rising. When a new band centre was opened by Canon Crowe PP in 1980, a harmonious future seemed in store for the green clad bandsmen of Blanchardstown.

Saint Brigid's church in Blanchardstown, with its unusual spire, was completed in 1856, replacing a building dating from penal times. The old building to the left of Saint Brigid's was, in 1828, a Carmelite convent and, for a short time in the 1850s, a junior seminary of the French Holy Ghost fathers who later established Blackrock College.

Abbotstown, to the north of Blanchardstown village, is also rich in historical associations. The area took its name from the Abbot family, who settled the land at the same time as the Blanchards. One of Ireland's wealthiest Catholic families, the Sweetmans, lived there in the 17th century until they were attainted as Jacobites in the 1690s and had their estate confiscated.

They were followed at Abbotstown by the Falkiner family, who were followed in turn by the Hamiltons. They acquired the lands in the early 19th century and three generations of Hamiltons represented Co. Dublin as MPs. In 1897, Ian Trant Hamilton was created First Lord Holmpatrick. In this century the government purchased the lands and a veterinary research laboratory was established. In July 1955 the James Connolly Dublin regional chest hospital was opened as part of the TB eradication campaign.

The lands of Corduff were held for centuries by the staunchly royalist Warren family, who suffered greatly under the Cromwellian regime in the 1650s. In the 18th century several members of the family entered the army of France and served in the Irish Brigade. William Warren and his step-brother John Warren, fought as captains in the Regiment of Lally at the great French victory over the British at Fontenoy in 1745. Later that year the brothers followed the Young Pretender, Prince Charles Edward, to Scotland and fought at Culloden, in 1746. After this disastrous defeat for Bonnie Prince Charlie the Warren brothers managed to escape back to France.

A younger brother, Richard Warren, also served in the Regiment of Lally and went to Scotland in 1745 as aide-de-camp to Lord George Murray, Bonnie Prince Charlie's general. He was later promoted and became an aide to the Prince himself. He was in France seeking reinforcements when news of the defeat at Culloden broke. A rescue mission for the Prince was immediately organised and Richard Warren, now a Colonel, was selected to lead it. After many narrow escapes Colonel Warren and the Prince, along with a number of followers, set sail from Loughnanaugh in the West of Scotland just before sunrise on October 3rd, 1746. They landed safely in France shortly afterwards.

Colonel Warren continued his distinguished career in the service of France, and in 1762, King Louis XV granted him the rank of Baron Warren of Corduff and Marcial de Camp. At the end of the Seven Years War in 1763 Baron Warren was appointed governor of Belleisle and its neighbouring islands, a post he held until he died on June 22nd, 1775.

BLANCHARDS - TOWN

At Fontenoy in 1745 the brothers William and John Warren of Corduff, Blanchardstown, fought on the side of French King Louis XV. as officers of the Irish Brigade.

Another brother, Col. Richard Warren who rescued Bonnie Prince Charlie after the failure of "45" was later made a Marshal of France.

Blanchardstown Band, Ireland's oldest village band was founded in 1826

J WREN

Blackrock

Carraig Dubh

The Dublin suburb of Blackrock became a fashionable seaside resort in the early 18th century and was so named from a rock of black limestone which once skirted the shoreline here.

Nothing remains of this rock today but it is believed that a portion of it lies buried beneath the Peoples Park and part of it was used in the building of the railway wall at Williamstown.

In celtic times this place formed part of the lands of Argortin, or the tillage lands, of which history records nothing of any interest. There is an ancient holy well called Tobernea near Seapoint Avenue which is said to be dedicated to Saint Naithí, after whom Taney or Teach Naithí was called. This area is known as Dundrum today.

We know nothing of the history of the ancient stone cross with the carved head which has stood for centuries in the Main Street of Blackrock. This ecclesiastical cross dates back to about the 10th century and in past times was used as the boundary mark by Dublin corporation when Riding the Franchises.

In the 13th century the lands of Blackrock became the property of Saint Mary's Abbey, Dublin, when they were presented to the monks by the Anglo-Norman lord of the district Raymond Carew. For three centuries the Cistercian monks and their tenants farmed these lands, until 1539 when they were confiscated and presented to Sir John Travers, the Kings Master of Ordnance in Ireland.

In the early 17th century the lands of Blackrock, or Newtown as they were then known, came into the possession of John Cheevers, a catholic who had married Katherine the daughter of Sir John Travers. After the Confederate wars of the 1640s the Cheevers family were dispossessed of their lands and exiled to Connaught, along with many others in similar circumstances.

In depth of the winter of 1653 Walter Cheevers, his wife, five children, his servants and retainers vacated the ancestral home and trekked across the country to find a new one in the wilds of the West of Ireland. The Cheevers estate was, however, returned after some years and in 1660, with the restoration of the Stuart monarchy to replace Cromwell's military government,

Walter Cheevers returned to Blackrock where he remained until his death in 1678.

The lands of Blackrock next passed to John Byrne, who married Cheevers daughter. As a result the area became known as Newtown Castle Byrne. Byrne was a barrister and sheriff of Co. Wicklow. He came from an old family of that county and was succeeded by his son John. Newtown Avenue takes its name from the estate.

During the early years of the 18th century, when Blackrock became the favourite seaside of Dubliners, many fine villas were built. On Sundays and holidays city folk thronged the village. The inns and places of entertainment did a roaring trade.

"The Three Tun Tavern" was a merry haunt and the "Sign of the Ship" with its spacious ballroom had its counterpart across the bay. For 18th century Fairview also had a "Sign of the Ship".

At "Conway's Tavern", which stood at the corner of Main Street and Georges Avenue, a melon festival was held annually. Medals were awarded to the producers of the best melons grown in the district.

Less pleasant activities sometimes preoccupied local residents however, as in 1787 when a meeting was held at "Jennetts Tavern" by the Blackrock Association to consider ways or ridding the area of highwaymen. Lord Ranelagh presided.

Many fine mansions were built in Blackrock during the georgian period. The redbricked Blackrock House is of particular note. It was erected in 1774 by John Lees, secretary of the Irish Post Office.

This three storied edifice was the summer residence of the Lord Lieutenants of Ireland for a number of years and many distinguished guests stayed here.

The Marquis of Buckingham, the Earls of Westmoreland and Camden, Lord Castlereagh and the equally infamous Earl of Clare were all visitors. When the Lord Lieutenants were in residence it was said that Blackrock revelled in "the sweets of dissapation to so high a degree that

even Bath could scarce take the lead for more gaiety, amusement and bon ton".

Frescati House was built about 1762 by the Hely Hutchinsons and became the residence of the Leinster family when Emily FitzGerald, Duchess of Leinster bought it in 1766. She immediately added two wings to the building and Lord Edward FitzGerald spent most of his childhood years here.

A younger son of the Duke, Lord Edward travelled widely. In 1793 he returned from France with his wife Pamela to live at Frescati. The mansion became an important setting for meetings of the United Irishmen.

Arthur O'Connor, Seamus McNevin and others visited Lord Edward regularly and Tom Paine (author of the "Rights of Man") called to Frescati to offer his young friend French aid. Sadly, Frescati House today is in a derelict state and awaiting demolition.

Maretimo was built a little later in 1774 and was demolished in the early 1970s to make way for a private flats complex. It was built by Nicholas Lawless, Lord Cloncurry, who was a leading merchant and MP for Lifford.

This square, brick house had nothing of great architectural merit but offered magnificent views of the bay. Nicholas Lawless was succeeded by his son Valentine, who in his youth was interned in the Tower of London for being a member of the United Irishmen.

Valentine Lawless, 2nd Baron Cloncurry, whose family estate was at Lyons, Co. Kildare, lived to the age of 84 years, when he died at Maretimo in 1853. Overlooking the nearby railway station, its proximity to the train services no doubt helped seal its fate for the developers in the 1970s.

Other handsome residences erected during this period included Rockfield, the seat of Edward Willes, Chief Baron of the Irish Exchequer, and Temple Hill House (then known as Neptune).

(Continued on Page 44)

BLACKROCK

BLACKROCK BECAME A FASHIONABLE SEASIDE RESORT IN THE EIGHTEENTH CENTURY WHEN THE ASCENDANCY CLASS BUILT THEIR SUMMER VILLAS THERE.

THE HISTORY OF THE ANCIENT STONE CROSS OF BLACKROCK IS NOT KNOWN. THE CROSS WAS RE-ERECTED ON A NEW BASE AFTER 1959 WHEN IT WAS TAKEN DOWN FOR ROAD — WIDENING.

FRESCATI HOUSE, BLACKROCK (NOW IN RUIN) WAS THE CHILDHOOD HOME OF LORD EDWARD FITZGERALD AND HE LIVED THERE WITH HIS WIFE PAMELA IN 1793

J.WREN '77

Cabra
(The Thicket)

It is generally believed that one of the five great roads of prechristian Ireland, that radiated from Tara passed through Cabra, although it is also thought it may have passed through Feltrim and followed the course of the present Malahide Road. What is not in dispute is that it continued on to Glendalough, in Co Wicklow.

Cabra itself is a much more recent creation. It received scant reference in D'Alton's 'History of County Dublin', which described it as "a well wooded demesne". In 1838, Cabragh Hill was first mentioned as part of the ploughland of Ballygossan granted to the Prior of Holmpatrick by King Edward I in the 13th century. In 1487 the inhabitants and landholders of Little Cabragh were, by Act of the Irish Parliament, made electors of Dublin city, although it wasn't until 1499 that the two districts of Little Cabragh and Much Cabragh were integrated into the city area.

Promixity to the city did not provide much security for the residents, who lived in the shadow of Sallcock's Wood. This stretched from present day Dalymount to the site of St Joseph's School for the Deaf on Rathoath Road. The district was regularly pillaged by the Wicklow septs. The best known local family as the Seagraves (or Sedgraves), from the Norse word Sio Greve, or Sea Lord. Several were leading members of the pre-reformation church and the judiciary.

Several were also soldiers, including Captain James Segrave who unhorsed Hugh O'Neill at the battle of Clontibret, which marked the opening of the great revolt of the Gaelic chieftains against Elizabeth I in 1595. Segrave a man of great personal courage and physical strength, attacked O'Neill in a desperate bid to reverse the English defeat. But one of O'Neill's retainers lopped off Segrave's arm as he was about to kill the rebel leader and O'Neill then despatched his opponent with a knife.

In the 17th century the Segraves resided at Cabra House and, in 1641, Henry Segrave owned 94 acres on the site. Despite their loyalty to the Crown the family remained staunchly "papish". In 1619 Walter Segrave left special provision for the maintenance of candidates for the priesthood in his will. His son was accused of sympathy with Catholic rebels, "priests, Jesuits and friars" during Cromwell's Commonwealth and had to flee. He received royal protection after the Restoration of Charles II.

Aras an Uachtarán, the former Vice Regal Lodge, was partially built on land formerly owned by the Segraves. In return Henry John Segrave was permitted to hunt nine deer annually in the Phoenix Park. A descendant, Sir Henry Segrave, was the holder of the world land speed record in the 1920s. He was killed in an effort to win the world water speed record on Lake Windermere, England, in 1930.

Perhaps the most notorious resident of old Cabragh was John Toler, Lord Norbury, the hanging judge who sentenced Robert Emmet to death. A former MP for Tralee, Norbury won his elevation to the peerage and became a Chief Justice by his slavish loyalty to the government of the day – whoever it happened to be. He rented Cabra House, an old Segrave rersidence, in 1791 and it is interesting to note that this Tudor building had been formerly described as "a notorious resort for priests", Jesuits and friars".

The convent of the Dominican nuns in the townland of Great Cabragh stands on the site of the house of Benedict Arthur, which is recorded in 1660 to have had six chimneys. Saint Mary's Dominican convent at Cabra was established in 1819 and houses primary and secondary school for emotionally disturbed children. During Pope John Paul II's visit to Ireland, in September 1979, he met physically and mentally handicapped people at the Cabra convent, which stands close to the Papal Nunciature. While at Cabra the Pope also conferred with the Catholic hierarchy and met leaders of other Irish religious denomination.

St Joseph's School for the Deaf, which is internationally renowned, was founded by Monsignor William Yore, parish priest of St Paul's, Arran Quay and Father Thomas McNamara of St Peter's, Phibsboro, in 1845. The original building was at Glasnevin but a new purpose-built school was begun at the junction of the Navan Road and the old Cabra Road on June 9th, 1856, when Archbishop Cullen laid the foundation stone. It was opened, under the management of the Christian Brothers, in the following year.

One of the world's greatest mathematicans, William Rowan Hamilton, had close associations with Cabra. He was appointed director of Dunsink Observatory, Castleknock in 1827, when only 22 years old. He frequently walked along the banks of the Royal Canal at Cabra and it was during one of these walks that he finally solved the problem of quarternions, a major breakthrough in mathematics, on October 16th, 1843. He celebrated the event with a commemorative stone on Broomebridge on which the crucial formula, $i2 = J2 = IJK = -1$ is engraved.

In October 1869 Cabra was the site of another very different historic event. Over 300,000 gathered to take part in an amnesty meeting for the Fenian prisoners. Amongst the speakers was Isaac Butt. The meeting provided the impetus for the founding of the Home Rule movement and the British prime minister Gladstone's reforms in Ireland. In 1882 Marlborough Barracks was built in Cabra at a cost of nearly £100,000. It was taken over by the Free State forces in December 1922 and renamed after Brigadier Dick McKee, the former O/C of the Dublin Brigade, IRA, who was murdered by British Auxiliaries on Bloody Sunday 1920. When Radio Eireann was set up in 1926 its first transmission mast was at McKee Barracks. Today it houses the Army School of Equitation and several other units.

In 1930 Dublin Corporation began building the huge housing estates in Old Cabra that were to transform the village into a suburb of the city. In 1939 work began in Cabra West and the families made homeless by the German bombing of the North Strand in 1941 were the first new residents there. It was during this period that Cabra also became a parish in its own right, distinct from Arran Quay and in October 1933 a new parish church, that of Christ the King, was opened.

CABRA

THE FENIAN AMNESTY MEETING AT DONNELLY'S FIELD CABRA WHICH WAS HELD ON OCTOBER THE 10TH 1869

THE HANGING JUDGE, LORD NORBURY LIVED FOR MANY YEARS AT CABRA HOUSE

IN 1534 A FORCE OF PALES-MEN WERE DEFEATED BY MEMBERS OF THE O'TOOLE SEPT IN SALLCOCKS WOOD CABRA

DOMINICAN CONVENT CABRA ESTABLISHED IN 1819

THE OLD CARDIFFS BRIDGE BETWEEN CABRA AND FINGLAS

J WREN

Castleknock

Castleknock was one of the greatest baronies of County Dublin. Bounded by Coolock and Nethercross on the north, Newcastle to the south, County Meath to the west and Dublin city to the east, it contained seven parishes, 74 townlands and just over 12,000 acres. In the 17th century most of the land enclosed to form the Phoenix Park by the Duke of Ormonde when he was viceroy was taken from the barony.

It takes its name from the legendary figure, Cnucha, variously described as one of the wives of Dela's five sons during the era of the Firbolgs and the foster mother of Conn of the Hundred Battles.

According to the Book of Lismore:
The nurse of Conn who lived this strip of land
Was Cnucha of the lovely head;
She dwelt on the dun with him
In the region of Conn of the Hundred Fights.
Cnucha, the daughter of Concadh Cas,
From the land of Luimneach broad and green,
Died yonder in that house
To the horror of the Gaels.
The woman was buried, a grief it was,
In the very middle of the hill;
So that from that on Cnucha
Is its name until the judgement.

As early as the Milesian era Cnucha is mentioned as one of 25 places at which Conmhaol, high king and leader of the race of Ebor, defeated the descendants of Eremon in battle. It was certainly a royal residence well before the birth of Conn of the Hundred Battles and his grandfather or great grandfather, Elim, son of Conn, is the first known ruler of the prechristian dun built there. His son Tuathal the Legitimate fought off an attack by rival chieftain Eochaid there and Conn of the Hundred Fights defeated Cumhall, the father of Finn in a victory commemorated in the poem 'The Battle of Cnucha'.

Apart from a reputed visit by St Patrick, it is rarely mentioned again in the annals before the Anglo-Norman invasion, but then assumed considerable importance as a military strongpoint of the invaders. The Tyrell family, whose forebears distinguished themselves at the Battle of Hastings, were given the lands and held them until the beginning of the 15th century, when the last of the male line died out.

During this period successive barons of Castleknock were confidants of English kings such as Richard the Lion Heart and Henry III. The sixth baron, Richard Tyrell, accompanied Edward I during his conquest of Scotland but later paid for the privilege when taken prisoner with his wife during Edward Bruce's invasion of Ireland 18 years later, in 1317. The couple had to pay a large ransome to secure their release. Richard was also in protracted litigation with the Priory of Kilmainham over the allowance of food promised to the monks from his estates and was threatened with imprisonment by the chief justice of Ireland when he failed to return one of the latter's favourite falcons.

Early in the 15th century Thomas Sergeant, a son of Joan Tyrell by her first marriage, succeeded to the estates of his grandfather Robert Tyrell and the estates quickly passed through marriage to Sir Nicholas Barnewall. By the beginning of the 16th century the land had passed to John Burnell, a supporter of Silken Thomas, the rebel earl of Kildare and was later attainted for treason with his master.

A relative, also called John Burnell, was granted the estate at Castleknock on a 45 year lease and it then passed on similar leases to various officers of the crown, including the marshal of the army, Lord Stanley in 1558, the attorney general Luke Dillon in 1568 and the Earl of Ormonde in 1574. However the Burnells appear to have kept ownership of the castle itself for many years and John Burnell's son Henry was reckoned one of the finest of 16th century lawyers. He frequently represented the interests of the great landlords of the Pale in their protests over heavy taxation by the crown and in 1577 was imprisoned in the Tower of London while arguing his clients' case with Queen Elizabeth I. Despite being a Catholic, he was made a judge in 1573 and rose to be a justice of

the queen's bench. He was later dismissed for drafting a petition requesting Catholic toleration from James I and ended his days as a skilled advocate in the courts and a thorn in the side of less competent judges who presided there. The family later moved to another estate at Castlerickard in County Meath.

During the wars of the 1640s the castle was initially occupied by rebels and it was only in 1642 that General Monk, one of the ablest commanders of the period, recaptured it for the crown and "killed 80 rebels besides those that were hanged" of the survivors. The rebels continued to control the surrounding countryside however and in November they captured a government convoy en route from Trim to Dublin, shooting their own prisoners afterwards. In 1647 the castle changed hands again, falling into the possession of Owen Roe O'Neill. It was to pass into the possession of the royalist leader Ormonde and the parliamentary forces of Oliver Cromwell before the wars of the confederacy of Kilkenny ended.

A survey carried out during the Commonwealth period of the 1650s showed the castle as having fallen into disrepair with a thatched house, a stable, some cottages and an orchard adjoining it. In the 'churchtown' nearby were listed another thatched house, a stable, some cottages, a disused mill and the walls of an old church.

After the restoration of the Stuarts in 1660 the settlement grew rapidly. Several leading landlords and city fathers bought properties in the area, there were 30 one hearth cottages in the two 'towns' and the mill, known as the Baron's Mill or the Red Mill, was reopened by a John Sprotton. The most important dwelling in the area was Porterstown, the home of Roger, first Earl of Orrery, when he was acting as a lord justice and in 1739 John

(Continued on Page 58)

CASTLEKNOCK

CASTLEKNOCK CASTLE WAS CONSTRUCTED AT THE BEGINING OF THE ANGLO-NORMAN INVASION BY HUGH TYRELL. IN 1171, THE HIGH KING RORY O CONNOR SET UP HIS H.Q. AT CASTLEKNOCK. IN 1317 EDWARD BRUCE CAPTURED THE CASTLE AND IN 1642 GENERAL MONK ANNIHILATED A CONFEDERATE FORCE THERE.

DEATH OF CNUCHA FOSTER MOTHER OF CONN OF THE HUNDRED BATTLES

BATTLE OF CNUCHA SECOND CENTURY A.D.

HUGH TYRREL FIRST BARON OF CASTLEKNOCK.

IN HIS "LIFE OF SAINT PATRICK (1180) THE MONK JOCELIN MENTIONS THE SAINT'S VISIT TO CASTLEKNOCK.

ST. BRIGID'S CHURCH OF IRELAND CASTLEKNOCK

J.WREN

Page 27

Chapelizod

Seipeil Izod

(Chapel of Isolde)

Overlooking the ancient village of Chapelizod, atop a hill called Knockmary in the Phoenix Park, stands a stone cromlech which attests to the existence of early man in this area. The Chapelizod place name is derived from Seipeil Izod, or the Chapel of Izod or Isolde the daughter of Aengus, the King of Ireland who according to tradition had a chapel here. Isolde, who flourished in the 6th century in the days of Arthur and the knights of the round table, was the heroine of one of the great European romantic sagas.

The love story of Tristan and Isolde has been immortalised down through the ages by poets and writers of many nations. From the Anglo-Norman Thomas of Brittany to the German, Gottfried Von Strassburgh, the Englishmen, Sir Thomas Malory and Sir Alfred Tennyson to Richard Wagner who based his opera "Tristan and Isolda" on the legend. The old church ruin in Mill Lane, Palmerstown is reputed to stand on the site of Dun Aengus where Tristan on behalf of King Mark of Cornwall asked King Aengus for the hand of Isolde in marriage. In times past there was a spring well in the vicinity of Kilmainham called Isolde's Font and an ancient tower which stood at Essex Quay until 1675 was known as Isolde's Tower.

After the Anglo-Norman invasion the lands of Chapelizod were retained as crown property and about 1170 Hugh De Lacy granted lands here to Hugh Tyrell. When the Knights Templars established their priory and hospital at Kilmainham, the Tyrells bestowed on them Chapelizod with all liberties in wood, meadow, pasture, water, mills and fisheries.

About 1200 King John leased lands at Chapelizod to Richard De La Field in whose family they remained for over two centuries. The Kilmainham priory held the manor of Kilmaihnam with the Kings fisheries and mill for several hundred years until 1476, when the manor was granted to Sir Thomas Daniel.

In the 16th century Robert Savage, crown yoeman and chief sergeant of county Dublin, was resident at Chapelizod and the north Dublin families, the Burnells of Balgriffin and the Bathes of Drumcondra, held lands here. In the 17th century Attorney General Sir John Davies and soldier Sir Henry Power, later created Viscount Valentia, resided at Chapelizod.

After his victory at the battle of the Boyne, William III stayed for some time at the old manor house of Chapelizod, which was known as the King's House. William of Orange issued three royal proclamations from "Our Court of Chapelizod" and had the grounds laid out in the Dutch style of planting. In the 17th and 18th centuries the King's House was home of Viceroys and the custodians of the extensive gardens here were placed on the civil list with a salary of £120 in 1717.

The King's House later became a military barracks and by the early 19th century was deserted. The beautiful garden then became a tangled mass of ruin. In the early part of this century Chapelizod dog-track occupied this site and today an industrial estate covers the area.

In the 17th century a stone-cutter and sculptor of renown, Edmund Tingham, lived at Chapelizod, his best known work was the "Marble Tomb of the Earl of Cork" in St. Patrick's Cathedral.

The Duke of Ormond, when Viceroy, lived in the King's house and directed one Colonel Richard Lawrence in establishing a linen factory at Chapelizod. This linen factory passed from Colonel Lawrence to the Lovett family, who were displaced for a time under James II in favour of a Quaker named Bromfield. In the 1700s Chapelizod was well known for its houses of entertainment, including "The Ship Tavern" and "The Three Tuns Grapes". In 1787 a Thomas Morris, publican, advertised good cheer and stabling for 60 horses. In 1761 Captain Richard Aylmer, a centenarian who had served under Charles II and James II, died at Chapelizod 105 years of age.

The Church of Ireland building of St. Lawrence is reputed to stand on the site of the Chapel of Isolde after which the village is named. The belfry tower of the church dates back to the late medieval period and is built around an earlier round one.

The present church, which was built in 1832, has many old tomb stones in the adjoining graveyard and General Vallency, designer of Queen St. Bridge, is buried here. The old house which stands in front of the church is the one referred to by Joseph Sheridan Le Fanu in his famous novel "The House by the Churchyard". Le Fanu, who spent his childhood years in the Royal Hibernian School, Phoenix Park, (where his father was Chaplain), knew the Chapelizod area well and many of his stories are set here.

KNOCKMAREE TUMULUS CHAPELIZOD

CHAPELIZOD

SEIPEIL ISOLDE — CHAPEL OF ISOLDE

CHAPELIZOD IS SAID TO HAVE BEEN THE RESIDENCE OF FAIR ISEULT, BELOVED OF TRISTAN, OF THE GREAT EUROPEAN LEGEND. THERE HAS BEEN MANY VERSIONS OF THE STORY OF TRISTAN AND ISOLDE THE MOST FAMOUS OF THEM ALL IS THE ONE WHICH RICHARD WAGNER USED FOR HIS OPERA OF THE SAME NAME.

THERE IS A LATE MEDIEVAL TOWER INCORPORATED IN THE PROTESTANT PARISH CHURCH OF ST. LAURENCE IN THE VILLAGE OF CHAPELIZOD.

WILLIAM OF ORANGE AND HIS COURT STAYED AT THE KINGS HOUSE CHAPELIZOD AFTER THE BATTLE OF THE BOYNE IN 1690.

J WREN '80

Clondalkin

Cluan Dolcan

(Dolcan's Pasture)

Clondalkin today is one of Dublin's newest satellite towns with housing estates and a modern industrial complex but the old village and famous round tower at the centre remain almost intact.

The ancient tower belonged to the monastery of St Cronan or Mochua and was styled bishop and abbot of Clondalkin. His pattern day is August 6th. One of the richest livings in the old Celtic church, Clondalkin was frequently the cause of dispute. In 1076 the clergy of Leath Mhoga led an army against the bishop, Fiachna Ua Ronain, who was said to have assumed office in violation of the right of a Maeldulau. The church and lands were then given to the Culdees and the disinherited successor was given compensation of 12 score cows. In the following century it became a prebend, or subsidiary of St Patrick's, the new Anglo-Norman cathedral in Dublin.

The mediaeval church built at Clondalkin was reputedly one of the finest in the country but was destroyed by a gunpowder explosion in a nearby mill in 1787. Ironically, the much earlier round tower opposite has survived in almost perfect condition. It is 84 feet high and still has its conical cap, plinth and outside stair preserved. The graveyard of the mediaeval church also contains two fine granite crosses and a granite baptismal font.

In the middle ages Clondalkin was a large and prosperous manor run for the church by a local bailiff and the archbishop of Dublin had one of his country residences there. It was frequently the target of raids from Wicklow. Yet at the end of the 14th century Clondalkin was described as a village with five streets, Mill Street, Steeple Street, Pope Lane, New Street and Mahow Street. A prominent local family in the 14th and 15th centures was the Neills, who claimed descent from the royal house of Ulster and gave their name to nearby Neilstown and also owned property in Dublin's New Street.

The Dean of St Patrick's at the time of the Reformation was Edward Bassenet, whom Swift later castigated as "the scoundrel who surrendered the Deanery to that beast Henry VIII". But he also secured for his own heirs the control of parts of the Clondalkin church lands at Deansrath and Nangor. These were only returned to the deanery of St Patrick's when the Bassenets retired to Britain during the turbulent years at the end of the 16th and 17th century.

Newlands became the principal residence in the vicinity of Clondalkin in the 17th century. It was initially the home of Samuel Molyneux, Queen Elizabeth I's Clerk of Works in Ireland and Daniel Molyneaux, her Ulster King of Arms. They were sons of Thomas Molyneaux, a former Chancellor of the Exchequer and brothers-in-law of Sir Newcomen in nearby Ballyfermot.

In the great rebellion of 1641 Clondalkin suffered severely. In January of 1642 the village was burnt by a troop of horse under Sir William Parsons, whose family owned Ballymount, and he advised the authorities in Dublin to raze Deansrath castle "to ease the town and to help free the country". By 1657 the Down Survey recorded that only a stump of a castle, some thatched houses and a round tower remained at Clondalkin. During the Commonwealth and Restoration period the ownership of the land underwent numerous changes but by the early 18th century the principal resident was Sir Arthur Cole at Newlands, the son of a prominent Cromwellian who was subsequently created Lord Ranelagh. The Browner family still held land and built a house near the village in 1714, while Mr Joseph Budden, one of the Commissioners for forfeited estates held Nangor Castle. Later his son-in-law John Falkiner of the famous Dublin banking family rebuilt the residence in Queen Anne style when he was High Sheriff of County Dublin.

The village was twice chosen as a site for gunpowder mills, both of which ended in catastrophes. The first was in 1733, when the mill blew up causing "several persons much damage". In 1782 a second mill was built at Moyle Pak. It was constructed by William Caldbeck, a leading reformer, distinguished barrister and Colonel of the lawyers' corps of the Irish Volunteers. He also built a foundry to manufacture brass cannon. The foundation stone of the gunpowder mill was laid by the Earl of Charlemont on May 1st 1782. The explosion in 1787 only caused the loss of two lives but the village was severely damaged and chimneys on houses as faraway as Usshers Quay in Dublin collapsed.

Two oil mills provided some employment in the late 18th century but the village then entered a period of decline. Its most distinguished resident was Arthur Wolfe, Viscount Kilwarden, who resided at Newlands. The most distinguished and humane member of the Irish bench in his day, he was tragically killed by a mob during Robert Emmet's shortlived rebellion of 1803.

John D'Alton in his History of County Dublin, published in 1838, described Clondalkin as "a neat little village" with "a smiling assemblage of cleanly cottages, interspersed with the venerable remains of other days". It was another 150 years before it became a major satellite town for Dublin.

In the last century one of the few sources of local employment were the calp quarries, which were located opposite the Red Cow on the Clondalkin side of the Naas Road. In Dutton's Survey of Co Dublin (1802) we read that the stone at the Red Cow was called Waller and it was said that the steps of St Paul's cathedral in London were made of it. Baldonnell, now Casement aerodrome, was built of stone from the Red Cow quarries between 1918 and 1920.

The Round Towers GAA club in Clondalkin is one of the oldest in the country and according to local tradition Michael Cusack, the first secretary of the Association, had a hand in its formation. Shortly after the historic Thurles meeting in 1884 Cusack, while walking in Clondalkin, came across a group of young footballers and suggested that they should start a GAA club and call themselves after the village's most famous landmark.

CLONDALKIN

In 865 the Viking fort of Dun Aulaff at Clondalkin was attacked by the King of Laois and its defenders were slain.

A monastery was founded at Clondalkin in the 7th century by St. Mochua (alias Cronan).

In 1787 an explosion at Corkagh Powder Mills caused much consternation for miles around.

J. Wren '82

Clontarf

Cluain Tarbh

(The Meadow of the Bull)

Three miles from Dublin city on the northern shore of the bay, where the once green moynalty sloped to the sea, lies the ancient district of Clontarf. Clontarf, or Cluain Tarbh meaning the meadow of the bulls, was so called because of the similarity between the sound of the thunderous sea and the bellowing of bulls.

The legendary people of Parthalon inhabited this district and the former existence of a number of tumuli along the seashore attest to early settlement here. These ancient burial mounds were perhaps part of Magh Dumha (the plain of the tumuli) where Brian Boru's tent stood during the Battle of Clontarf. There is a tradition that the High King's tent was placed on high ground where St. Lawrence's Road runs today.

Clontarf was associated with Saint Comgall of Bangor during the early Christian period. He founded a church here in 550. Comgall, who was descended from Conel Cearnach, founded the monastery of Bangor and many others around Ireland. As a leader of the early Irish church he framed many monastic rules.

Saint Aidan of Clontarf, who is commemorated in the Martyrology of Tallaght, was in all probability a member of the community but nothing is known of the history of this foundation. It is presumed that the ruined church in the graveyard on Castle Avenue stands on the site of Comgall's monastery.

On Good Friday, 23rd April, 1014, one of the longest and bloodiest battles to have been fought on Irish soil took place on the plain of Clontarf. Here along the shoreline of Dublin bay a Norse and Leinster-Irish force was defeated by the combined armies of Munster and Connaught on a field of appalling carnage. Here the High King, Brian Boru, was killed by the axe blow of a fleeing Viking while at prayer in his tent at the moment of final victory.

The discovery of quantities of human bones and weapons during the building of Dublin's north georgian city during the 18th and early 19th centuries led to the belief that the site of the battle was around the Mountjoy Square and Cavendish Row areas. The fishing weir where Brian's grandson Turlough was drowned was transposed to the Tolka, near Ballybough.

These locations, and others as far afield as Finglas, which are given for the site of the battle are all conjectures. There is no evidence extant that the district of Clontarf ever extended beyond the southern banks of the Tolka.

Undoubtedly the site of the fishing weir mentioned in the battle was at Clontarf itself. There was a salmon weir at a gravel bank called The Furlong opposite Vernon Avenue where men caught fish from time immemorial until early this century.

The main site of the conflict stretched along the seafront from Fairview to Dollymount, and inland as far as Artane and the Marino demesne. Before the commencement of housing development there was an area known as the "Bloody Fields" in Marino and it was probably here that the battle raged most fiercely.

In 1172 King Henry II granted Clontarf to the military order of the Knights Templars who built a commandery here. After the Templars were suppressed in 1309 the manor of Clontarf passed to the Order of the Knights of St. John of Jerusalem. They remained here until the dissolution of the monasteries by Henry VIII.

The last prior of Clontarf was Sir John Rawson who, on surrendering possession of the house in 1541, was created Viscount Clontarf with a pension of 500 marks. It is generally accepted that the original perceptory of the Knights Templars stood on the site of the present Clontarf castle. But there are some who hold that it was sited where the Manor House stood at the northern end of Castle Avenue.

During the rebellion of 1641 a force under Luke Netterville raided a ship for arms as it lay anchored at Clontarf and this resulted in the burning of the town by Sir Charles Coote. The Manor House of Clontarf, which was then occupied by a George King, was also burned by Coote, who has been described as the most ferocious and bloodthirsty soldier of the time.

It was alleged that part of the ship's cargo plundered by Netterville was found in King's home, for which the latter was attainted and a reward of £400 offered for his head. The manor of Clontarf then passed to John Blackwell, a friend of Oliver Cromwell.

He, in turn, transferred his interest to John Vernon, Quarter Master General of Oliver Cromwell's army in Ireland. The Vernons were descended from a Norman family who came to England with William the Conqueror.

They remained landlords of Clontarf for three centuries, until the failure of the male line. The Vernon estate passed to the Oulton family who sold their interest and Clontarf castle became a hostelry in 1957.

This fine building was rebuilt in the Norman style in 1835, to the design of William Vetruvius Morrison, a leading Irish architect. The reason was that the ancient edifice then standing was declared unsafe.

The old fishing village of The Sheds at Clontarf, situated at the present day junction of Vernon Avenue with the seafront, was so called because sheds were erected here in the 17th century for the purpose of drying and curing fish.

In 1787 Charles Weekes, a local resident, at his own expense diverted a stream running through his land to a reservoir for public use. He also built a wharf extending several hundred feet into the sea. It carried a water supply for the convenient use of shipping anchored in the pool of Clontarf.

Weekes' Wharf was a popular promenade for Dubliners on summer evenings. Seating was provided on a platform, which was a considerable distance out into the sea.

In the early 19th century the village at The Sheds became a popular seabathing resort for north city dwellers and many boarding houses were opened. The public house, now known as The Sheds, was opened in 1845 by James Gerald Mooney. He later went on to found the biggest chain of public

(Continued on Page 42)

CLONTARF · CLUAIN TARBH
MEADOW OF THE BULL

TOWARDS THE END OF THE BATTLE OF CLONTARF WHICH RAGED FOR TWELVE HOURS ON GOOD FRIDAY 1014, KING BRIAN BORU WAS SLAIN BY THE VIKING BRODIR WHILE AT PRAYER IN HIS TENT.

BEFORE THE NORTH LOTTS WAS RECLAIMED FROM THE SEA CLONTARF ISLAND WAS A PROMINENT LANDMARK IN DUBLIN BAY. IN 1650 CLONTARF ISLAND WAS A PLACE OF REFUGE WHEN A PLAGUE SWEPT THROUGH DUBLIN.

CLONTARF CASTLE WAS REBUILT IN 1835 AND STANDS ON THE SITE OF A MEDIAEVAL COMMANDERY OF THE KNIGHTS TEMPLAR

J.WREN '79

Coolock

An Culóg

(The Little Corner)

When John D'Alton published his history of County Dublin in 1838 he referred to several raths or mounds in the neighbourhood of Coolock. Some of them were still discernible but were much cut down and mixed with the soil of surrounding fields.

Of these raths, or burial mounds, only one now survives in the grounds of the Cadburys factory. It may date to the time of the destruction of the people of Parthalon by plague.

Probably the Gniomh Tamhlacht, meaning the plague mound of the twelfth part of a ploughland, mentioned in the early fifteenth century marriage dowry of Elizabeth Hollywood of Artane, is the same mound.

As recently as 1932 a tumulus in Bonnybrook, near the Santry river, was levelled and a large quantity of skulls and other human remains unearthed. The spot is marked on the ordnance survey map as the site of the burials.

One explanation for the concentration of mounds in the area is the theory that one of the five historic roads of Ireland, the Slighe Cualann which stretched from Tara down to Wicklow, passed through Garristown, Mullaghoo, Feltrim, Coolock and Artane — and on to Dublin.

With the coming of christianity to Ireland a small wattle church was built in Coolock. Today a primitive stone cross from this period still stands in the churchyard of St. John the Baptist, the Church of Ireland building which occupies the site of the ancient celtic church of St. Brendan the Navigator at the end of the Tonlegee Road.

There is no record of Saint Brendan ever having visited Coolock but a holy well bearing his name was for centuries a place of pilgrimage. Today a whitethorn bush marks its site near the present C. of I. structure.

The nearby Santry river probably gained its name slightly later. The stretch running between Coolock Bridge and Raheny became known as the Skillinglas - probably a Norse-Irish word meaning a boundary (Skil or Skyl) stream (glas). The name also stuck to the adjacent townland.

During Norman times Coolock was the property of the Nugent family. In 1207 Hacket De Nugent was already exercising proprietorial rights when he brought court proceedings for an ejectment.

The church at Coolock was under the patronage of Baron de Nugent until 1275, when it was appropriated by the Prior of Llanthony, the great Cistercian monastery in Gloucestershire. Later Coolock passed under the control of the monastery of Duleek and then the patronage of the Earl of Drogheda.

Following the reformation, the first small chapel to be built in Coolock was in 1689 during the brief interval of relaxation of the laws against catholics. However it was closed shortly afterwards with the enactment of the Penal Laws.

Yet by 1780, when the antiquary Austin Cooper visited the area, he observed a very large Roman chapel in a village consisting entirely of cabins. In 1831 the chapel was rebuilt and the old thatched roof replaced with slates at a cost of £500, an astronomic sum at the time.

By this time Coolock was a district noted for its rich agricultural produce, with which it supplied Dublin city. Originally the area had been covered by thick woods.

During the 17th and 18th centuries there was also a busy quarrying industry. In September 1764 the *Freeman's Journal* reported an injury to a workman at Coolock quarry. He was taken to Inns Quay infirmary for treatment.

A famous name linked with the area from this period is that of Henry Grattan (who was born at Belcamp Park). Coolock had its own corps of Irish Volunteers in the 1780s. Known as the Coolock Independents, they were commanded by Captain James Walker. There was also a Barony of Coolock Volunteer body under the command of Captain Richard Talbot.

The radical politics of the area surfaced again in 1803, during the Emmet rising. When Robert Emmet rose in rebellion his followers from all over north county Dublin gathered on the green near the present protestant church at Coolock, where they were joined by insurgents from County Meath. They were waiting for a signal to march on Dublin from Coolock, but alas it never came!

Meanwhile the same period saw a number of big houses built in Coolock. Coolock House itself dates from this time.

Now the residence of the Sisters of Mercy, in the last decade of the 18th century it was the home of William Callaghan, a Dublin chemist. In the year of Emmet's rising Callaghan adopted a young Dublin orphan girl of gentle disposition as a companion for his ailing wife.

Liberal protestants by tradition, the Callaghans encouraged the girl, Catherine McAuley, to practice her catholic religion and help the poor of Coolock. Catherine taught the catechism to local children in the gate lodge.

When William Callaghan died in 1822 he left his entire fortune to Catherine. Five years later she founded the first Convent of Mercy school and girls' hostel in Lower Baggot Street.

Another old Coolock house occupied by an order of nuns is the Holy Rosary convent, Springdale Road, which is a rest home for sisters on leave from the missions. Overlooking the Santry river, which flows through its grounds, this fine building was originally known as Brookville House.

One of the most modern structures in Coolock, Cadburys factory, stands on the site of Moatfield House. This was built by James Lever, an English architect who had been employed by Gandon on the building of the Custom House.

Moatfield was named after the moat, or mound, that can still be seen in the factory's grounds.

Another occupant of Moatfield was James Lever's son Charles, the famous novelist who spent his childhood there. Later he was to introduce into his writings many of the features of north-east Dublin.

The next occupant was Michael Staunton, the proprietor of the *Morning Register* and *Evening Herald* newspapers. A friend and

(Continued on Page 36)

COOLOCK

An Culóg — LITTLE CORNER

IN 1803 A GREAT CONCOURSE OF PEOPLE ASSEMBLED AT COOLOCK AND AWAITED A SIGNAL TO MARCH INTO DUBLIN TO JOIN IN ROBERT EMMETS REBELLION.

THE TUMULUS IN THE GROUNDS OF CADBURY'S FACTORY AT COOLOCK MAY BE THE PLAGUE MOUND WHICH IS LISTED IN 15TH CENTURY DOWRY OF ELIZABETH HOLLYWOOD OF ARTANE

COOLOCK HOUSE (NOW PART OF THE CONVENT OF VIRGO CLEMENS) WHERE MOTHER CATHRINE McAULEY LIVED FROM 1803 UNTIL 1826 AS THE ADOPTED DAUGHTER OF MR. AND MRS. CALLAGHAN

J. WREN '81

Crumlin

Cruimghlinn

(The Crooked Glen)

Crumlin or the Cruimghlinn was so called in ancient times after the crooked glen which is now the Landsdowne Valley. From the bardic tales we learn that the Fenian hero Ossian went to reside in Crumlin in his old age. Within the parish of Crumlin, in the townland of Greenhills, many cists and stone age burials were found and the urns they contained were deposited in the National Museum.

During the reign of King John the lands of Crumlin became one of the crown manors near Dublin, the others were Saggart, Newcastle Lyons, and Esker. The tenants of this manor were subject to many attacks over the centuries by raiders from the Wicklow hills. In 1331 after a foray in Tallaght the O'Tooles led a pursuing party in a trap at Culiagh near Crumlin where they set upon them, killing some prominent inhabitants of the district, including a Bret of Rathfarnham and two Barnwalls of Drimnagh.

In the 16th century Crumlin was raided on a number of occasions by the O'Byrnes and in 1594 members of this clan under the command of Walter Fitzgerald descended upon the manor in a night attack. The village and the church were plundered and burned and the lead from the roof of the building was taken away to make bullets. The following years the rebel Fiach MacHugh O'Byrne of Glenmalure, chief of the clan, in his last recorded raid again burned the village of Crumlin.

Two days after the battle of the Boyne, William of Orange and his victorious army camped on the common of Crumlin before they proceeded to the south of Ireland. The common of Crumlin was once again the popular venue for annual horse race meetings but, due to the efforts of irate local inhabitants, they were finally stopped in 1818 when the common was enclosed by an Act of Parliament.

The ancient Irish game of hurling was played on Crumlin common long before the foundation of the G.A.A. and there are several 18th century newspaper reports of such activities here. In May 1748 a Leinster selection defeated twenty Munster men in a grand match of hurling on Crumlin common and, in a return game a month later, they again emerged victorious. This happening was almost 200 years before·the inauguration of the Railway Cup competitions.

During the 14th and 15th centuries some of the leading religious houses in Dublin acquired lands in Crumlin and these included the Abbey of St. Thomas, the Priory of the Holy Trinity, the Cathedral of St. Patrick and St. Mary's Abbey. These possessions were held until the Dissolution.

In 1609 Edmund Purcell leased land at Crumlin and his descendants remained here until the 19th century. The Lord Mayor of Dublin in 1605, John Brice, was a resident of Crumlin. In the second half of the 17th century a portion of the Crumlin lands came into the possession of Major Joseph Deane, an officer in Cromwells army, who rose to high position in Ireland. It is said that Captains Road is called after this military man, his grandson, also a Joseph Deane, rose to the position of Chief Baron of the Exchequer during the reign of George I.

During the rebellion of 1798 several inhabitants of Crumlin suffered much loss and damage at the hands of the insurgents, particularly Arthur Orde and Thomas Jones who kept a boarding school there. When Robert Emmet led his abortive rising four years later Arthur Orde raised a company of infantry in the district to protect the property.

The Protestant church of St. Mary the Virgin at Crumlin stands on the site of a 12th century church of the same dedication. The church with its square tower was restored in the 18th century and, at the rere of it, is a modern church which was constructed with yellow brick from the former brickfields on the Crumlin Road. The 18th century chapel served the Catholic population of Crumlin until St. Agnes Church opened on Sunday 10th February 1935. This was built of Dublin granite and was in the Irish Romanesque style.

1935 saw the first 90 families move into what was then Dublin's newest town on the newly named Sundrive Road. Six months previously it had been an obscure country byway called the Dark Lanes. Over the next decade the tillage fields of Crumlin which had for centuries supplied the Dublin markets with fresh vegetables, became a vast housing estate, the domicile for thousands of Dublin families.

COOLOCK

(Continued from Page 34)

political associate of Daniel O'Connell, Staunton became Lord Mayor of Dublin in 1847 and O'Connell was a frequent visitor to Moatfield.

Staunton is believed to have erected a beautiful dining room for the reception of his famous guest. A protestant by religion, Staunton supported the struggle for catholic emancipation and also established a benefit society for Coolock in 1832, to help unemployed and sick workers.

Another "big house" in the area was Annesley Lodge, built by Lord Annesley in an estate of 34 acres on the Malahide Road. Early in the 19th century it came into the possession of General Cuppage, of Mount Edwards, Co. Antrim. A humane employer, General Alexander Cuppage assisted the destitute and poor labourers of Coolock during the worst years of the Famine.

A newspaper report of November 1846 described him as a "noble and generous heart who sympathised with woes and miseries of his fellow men. The gallant and venerable General Cuppage always treated his labourers in the most kind and humane manner. He gave them gardens and houses free of rent, paying them weekly wages without deductions whatsoever"

Clare Grove, the resident of General Cuppage, became in the 1960s the Clare Manor Hotel. It came to a sad end on the night of November 5th 1980 when it was burnt to the ground following a disco.

CRUMLIN
THE CURVED GLEN

WICKLOW INSURGENTS UNDER THE LEADERSHIP OF WALTER FITZGERALD BURNED THE CROWN MANOR OF CRUMLIN TO THE GROUND IN 1594.

HURLING WAS PLAYED ON CRUMLIN COMMON DURING THE 18TH CENTURY.

THE PARISH CHURCH OF ST. MARY (CHURCH OF IRELAND) CRUMLIN STANDS ON THE SITE OF A TWELFTH CENTURY CHURCH DEDICATED TO OUR LADY.

Dalkey

Deilig Inis

(Thorn Island)

Dalkey is one of the oldest settlements in Ireland and, during the middle ages it was the country's main port.

The first reference to the island itself is in the Annals of the Four Masters, who mention it in the division of Ireland between Heremon and Hebor. The earliest archaeological finds indicating human occupation have been carbon dated to around 3340 BC and predate the ancient kingdoms of Egypt and the Middle Ages.

The first reference to the island itself is in the Annals of the Four Masters, who mention it in the division of Ireland between Heremon and Hebor. The earliest archaeological finds indicating human occupation have been carbon dated to around 3,340 BC and predate the ancient kingdoms of Egypt and the Middle East.

By the eighth century AD references to the island are frequent and it boasted two churches. Both were named after St. Begnet, who was a local virgin saint. One was built on Dalkey island and the other on the adjoining mainland. Sections of the two churches still stand. The one on the mainland adjoins the main street in Dalkey village.

Used as a viking base in the tenth century, Dalkey island was uninhabited during the middle ages. On the mainland however, Dalkey harbour developed into a thriving port. The Normans first discovered its commercial potential when the sandbars in Dublin bay made the old viking port there unsafe for the larger merchant ships now being built. The sheltered sound between Dalkey island and the mainland (known as St. Begnet's Sea in the middle ages) were 30 fathoms deep, sheltered and easily defended.

No less than six castles, or fortified warehouses, were built to protect Dalkey and its rich cargoes. Walls were built to the east, west and north, while a great ditch was constructed to the south, which is still referred to by local people as 'The ramparts'.

Only two castles are still standing. One is the Goat Castle, which is the present rates office. It is named from the demi-goat in the coat of arms of the Chievres family who built it. Almost opposite on the main street is its only surviving companion, Archbold's castle.

Goods from vessels in the sound were landed in small boats at Dalkey and Bullock harbours. The Cistercian monks who owned St. Mary's Abbey in Dublin also owned the land around Bullock and built a castle there. Fish from Dalkey were regularly transported to Dublin for sale in the Fishamble area of the city.

Another Cistercian castle at Monkstown had an 'ice plant' in the dungeons to keep the fish fresh. But most goods took the main route to Dublin, along the route of the present Barnhill and Upper Glenageary roads. Mart Lane in Foxrock derives its name from a market held there by Dalkey merchants en route for the city.

Dalkey continued to thrive until the end of the seventeenth century, when Dublin corporation channelled the Liffey and began to improve the port's approaches.

During the late eighteenth century Dalkey island became the seat of a burlesque court presended over by "his facetious majesty the king of Dalkey, Emperor of Muglin's and Elector of Lambay and Ireland's Eye, Defender of his own faith and respector of all others, sovereign of the illustrious Order of the Lobster and Periwinkle". Up to 20,000 people used to attend the annual coronations.

A little later a martello tower was erected on the island and the garrison were the first permanent inhabitants for many centuries. Due to an oversight at the War Office in London, the garrison wasnever disbanded and the troops continued to be paid until the late nineteenth century, when most of them had either left or died of old age.

Ironically, Dalkey owed its revival in the early nineteenth century to a decision to build a major new port at Dun Laoghaire during the Napoleonic wars. Most of the granite for the project was mined from Dalkey. A three mile long railway took the rock down to the new port, with the weight of the full trucks (carrying 20 tons each) pulling the empty ones back up the hill to be refilled.

Most of the labourers employed in the quarries camped on Dalkey commons. When the work dried up, with the completion of Dun Laoghaire, most of them had acquired squatters rights, but they were bought out by property speculators anxious to acquire prime residential sites. The Metals, as the railway route is dubbed by local people, is still in existence and provides a pedestrian footpath into the centre of Dun Laoghaire.

The extension of the railways to Dalkey made it easily accessible from Dublin. Between 1844 and 1854, the service was provided by the world's first commercially successful atmospheric railway. It was only dismantled when the line was incorporated into the developing national rail network.

From 1830 the town was also served by a horse omnibus. Later a horse tram operated along cast iron rails until 1901, when the famous No. 8 electric tram linked Dalkey to the terminus at Nelson's Pillar in O'Connell Street. This service ceased, regrettably, in 1949.

One of the earliest of the buildings erected in Dalkey's nineteenth century revival was The Queen's Royal Hotel in 1820, which is still in business beside the Goat Castle. The Church of the Assumption, erected in 1840 stands almost opposite. It was Dalkey's first Catholic church.

Behind it are several large houses, one of which, Tudor House, was the site of a private school called Roothams College, where James Joyce taught briefly. The other literary figures associated with Dalkey are, of course, George Bernard Shaw and modern playwright Hugh Leonard.

In 1838 the Loreto nuns set up a school at Bullock Castle and bought up many properties in the area, including the impressive Carrige na Greinne from the Weir family. The house was built in 1820 and has extensive lands. The Weirs hoped to sell it to the local authority as a park, but the council couldn't afford it. The main fear today is that more speculative building will destroy the area's great natural beauty and amenity value.

DALKEY
THORN ISLAND

DURING THE MIDDLE AGES DALKEY WAS THE BUSY PORT OF DUBLIN AND WAS A PLACE OF GREAT COMMERCIAL ACTIVITY

IN THE EIGHTEENTH CENTURY A MOCK CORONATION CEREMONY WAS INSTITUTED WHEN THE MERRY MONARCH THE KING OF DALKEY ISLAND WAS CROWNED.

JWREN 79

GEORGE BERNARD SHAW SPENT HAPPY CHILDHOOD YEARS AT TORCA COTTAGE IN DALKEY AND LATER WROTE THAT THE SKIES THERE WERE MORE BEAUTIFUL THAN EVEN VENICE.

Donnybrook

Domhnach Broc   (The Church of Broc)

Donnybrook (The Church of Broc) is the site of an ancient monastic settlement on the banks of the Dodder which was founded by a holy woman called Broc about A.D. 750. This holy woman, who was one of the seven daughters of Dallbronach of Desii of Bregia, north county Dublin, built her church here and dedicated it to the Blessed Mother of God. The old graveyard in Donnybrook village marks its site.

Saint Mobi, who is mentioned in the Martyrology of Donegal, was a member of this community and was in the past a patron saint of this district. Some scholars hold that the great house of hospitality of Da Derga, where Conor Mór the High King of Ireland met his death in the century before Christ, stood at Donnybrook. But others claim that Bohernabreena was the site of the famous hostel.

After the Anglo-Norman conquest these lands, which had been previously held by the gaelic Mac Gillamocholmog clan, were granted to Walter De Ridelford, Lord of Bray and foremost follower of Strongbow. When De Ridelford died his inheritance went to his grand daughter Christina De Marisco. Then an infant she was bethrothed at the age of two to her appointed guardian, one Fulk of Newcastle. Having avoided marriage to Fulk she was forced to wed at the age of nine years Ebulo De Geneve. Later, having escaped to the protection of Eleanor, widow of Henry II, on the Continent she entered a convent and relinquished her estate to the crown.

In 1254 Lord Edward Baggod, or Baggot, the King's Deputy acquired land in the Donnybrook area and built a strong fort or Castle at a place called Baggot Rath. He was instrumental in establishing the Order of White Friars in Whitefriar Street. Toward the end of the 15th century the Baggot family left the castle of their ancestors and were succeeded there by another Norman family, the Fitzwilliams.

In 1524 when Alison Fitzwilliam married Christopher Ussher, she received Donnybrook as a marriage settlement and, after her death, her son John succeeded her to these lands. This John Ussher became a Lord Mayor of Dublin and built a large mansion house at Donnybrook, which later was called Donnybrook Castle. He was the first person to publish a book in the Irish language. It was the translation of the Catechism of the Established Church in 1571.

When Donnybrook Castle fell into the hands of the Stoyte family both Dean Swift and Stella were frequent visitors there. The castle eventually became ruinous and a smaller house was built on its site in 1798. This was called the Castle School of Donnybrook. In 1837 Mother Mary Aikenhead, foundress of the Irish Sisters of Charity, purchased the house with its adjoining grounds and it became the St. Mary Magdelen Home of Refuge. Later a chapel and laundry were added.

The earliest charter relating to the famous Donnybrook Fair goes back to 1204, when King John granted to the citizens of Dublin the right to hold an annual eight day fair in the village. The fair was originally held in May but it later extended to 15 days. It began on the 26th August each year. For centuries the Fair of Donnybrook ranked highly among the great European fairs as an important trading centre and merchants travelled here from many foreign countries to transact their business. Along with the various commodities, livestock, and farm produce sold at the fair, craftsmen, physicians, apothecaries, goldsmiths and moneydealers held stalls here.

The Bective Rangers rugby club ground now occupies the site of one portion of the original green fair and the C.I.E. garage on the opposite side of the main road the other. The importance of the commercial fair however gradually diminished and it was replaced by a fun fair when, at the end of the 17th century, the Corporation conveyed the right to collect the tolls of the Ussher family. The fair then degenerated into a wild and riotous assembly and for over a century it was the scene of drunkeness and outrage until it was finally suppressed in 1859.

At this time many fairs and patterns disappeared due to changing social habits and the expansion of the city's suburbs.

BALDOYLE

(Continued from Page 10)

Baldoyle was a fishing village up until the turn of the century. Nine fishing wherries operated from it and were crewed by eight or nine men each. In past centuries Baldoyle's small harbour gave accommodation for the coal trade, and one Barnaby Barrett had a shipowners and coal factors business here in 1805.

As late as 1837 there was a hedge school at Baldoyle catering for 12 pupils, according to Lewis's "Topographical Dictionary of Ireland". The same work informs us "that the village was then a chief station of the constabulary police and there was also a coastguard station".

In the last century Baldoyle was a very popular bathing resort for Dubliners, who thronged to it during the summer months. In 1887 James Warren of Baldoyle died at the age of 167 years, the oldest man on record to live in Ireland. James was, no doubt, a local character who drew the interest of the holidaymakers.

For over 100 years Baldoyle was celebrated for its fine racecourse and steeplechase. Unfortunately this was closed down in 1972 when the last meeting was held. Baldoyle racecourse was also the venue of several international athletic cross-country championship meetings. The earliest of these was held in 1905. Ireland's first success in this event was accomplished in 1931 by Tim Smyth from O'Callaghan's Mills, Co. Clare, when he became world cross country champion at Baldoyle.

With rapid housing development and a great increase in population since 1970, the Baldoyle of the little fishing fleet and green pastures is all but a forgotten memory.

DONNYBROOK
CHURCH OF BROC

THE FAMOUS FAIR OF DONNYBROOK WAS ESTABLISHED BY ROYAL CHARTER IN 1204 AND FOR 600 YEARS WAS RENOWNED THE WORLD OVER. THIS HISTORIC FESTIVAL WHICH HAD EVOLVED INTO A DISREPUTABLE AFFAIR WAS FINALY SURPRESSED IN 1855.

A CHURCH WAS FOUNDED AT DONNYBROOK AT THE END OF THE 8TH CENTURY BY A HOLY WOMAN NAMED BROC WHO WAS ONE OF THE SEVEN DAUGHTERS OF DALLBRONACH OF THE DESII OF BREGIA, CO. MEATH.

CHURCH OF THE SACRED HEART DONNYBROOK

DONNYBROOK CASTLE

Donnycarney

Domhnach Cearnach   (The Church of Cearnach)

According to the Tripartite Life of St. Patrick all the churches bearing the name Domnach were originally founded or pointed out by that Saint on Sundays (Domnach-Dominica-Sunday) and there is a tradition that St. Patrick founded such a church at Donnycarney near Dublin city. Near Mornington, Co. Meath, there is also a Donacarney which, like its Dublin counterpart, may have been dedicated to Saint Cearnach, a disciple of Patrick. A native of Cornwall Cearnach was the founder of Dulane near Kells, Co. Meath. There were several other holy men however, who have been known by this name and the 6th century Louthman, St. Carnach, grandson of Colgan, king of the territory, may have been the founder of one, or both, of these establishments.

Gentle Segnat, the virgin of Domnach Ceirne, is a hazy figure, a holy woman of whom nothing is known, except that her feast day fell on 18th December and that she resided at Donnycarney during the early years of the Celtic Church. Although there has been no trace of an ancient church found in the Donnycarney area the Annals of the Four Masters inform us that in the year 1106 Domhnall, the Archbishop of Armagh, was carried in his death sickness to Domnach Aithir Eamhna (the Church east of Navan) and there annointed. John O'Donovan the celebrated scholar and translator of the Annals has identified this place with Donnycarney, three miles north of Dublin City, but there has been disagreement as to its location since O'Donovan's time.

During the historic battle of Clontarf some fierce fighting took place in the Donnycarney - Marino district and there was formerly in the Marino area some ground called the ''Bloody Fields'' which was traditionally linked with the Marathon of Ireland. After the Norman invasion the church at Donnycarney seems to have disappeared, for the Creidi Midhi, the oldest existing record of the state of Dublin parishes, which dates to 1275, does not list it. In the 12th

century when Dermot McMurrough, the king of Leinster, founded the great Augustinian Priory of All Hallows on the site of the present Trinity College he granted to the monks the lands of Clonturk, Baldoyle and Donnycarney.

From the Donnycarney lands which then included Marino (a placename which only dates from the 18th century), the monks drew their supply of grain for centuries. From the register of All Hallows we learn that in 1240 John Lattimer of Coolock was involved in a dispute with the Canons of the Priory over a parcel of land in Donnycarney called Inchehaven. Inchehaven, meaning the water meadow, is today the ground covered by Collins Avenue East, under which the culverted Hollybrook stream passes.

After the dissolution of the monasteries, the rich lands of Donnycarney were granted by the king to the Corporation, who in turn leased them to James Stanyhurst, the recorder of Dublin and speaker in three Irish Parliaments under Mary and Elizabeth. In 1570 Christopher Hetherington was the occupier of Donnycarney and his family was still in residence at the time of the 1641 rebellion. In 1648 Colonel Michael Jones, Governor of the city and victor of the battle of Rathmines, at his own request to the Corporation, received

a lease of the Donnycarney lands. But he did not enjoy a long sojourn there for he died in the following year.

William Basil who, during the years of the Commonwealth, was Attorney General in Ireland, was the next owner of Donnybrook and was rated in 1667 for possessing a house there containing 15 hearths. In the early years of the 18th century George Berkeley, the philosopher, visited his friend Sir John Perceval on a number of occasions at Donnycarney House. He described the walk from Trinity College as a lovely one and the surroundings of Donnycarney as beautiful.

When Lord Charlemont, the Volunteer Earl, went to reside in his new georgian house on the lands of Donnycarney in 1750, he called it and the adjoining lands, Marino, because of their proximity to the sea. All that remains today of Charlemont's demesne is the magnificent little Casino. In the 1920s housing estates were built at Marino and Donnycarney, the first such schemes under an Irish government. The fine modern church of Our Lady of Consolation of Donnycarney (built in 1969) stands on grounds where, perhaps, pilgrims trod in the long ago to the temple of Domnach Airthir Eamhna, the church of Cearnach.

CLONTARF

(Continued from Page 32)

houses in Ireland. As well as a number in the Dublin area, Mooney's pubs were well known as far afield as Cork, Belfast and even London.

The foundation stone of the handsome Roman catholic church of St. John the Baptist at The Sheds was laid by Archbishop Murray in 1835. It was on the site which had previously been covered by a fishermen's settlement

It is interesting to note that the famous convict priest, Father Harold, was appointed administrator of Clontarf parish in 1818, after his return from Australia. He had been transported to Botany Bay in 1798 for sheltering a wounded rebel.

Canon Rooney, who was parish priest between 1846 and 1879 had witnessed the execution of Robert Emmet, as a child, in Thomas Street during 1803. In 1839 Father Edward McCabe was appointed curate at Clontarf. In later years he became archbishop of Dublin.

Conquer Hill, connected by tradition with the battle of Clontarf, was the venue chosen by Daniel O'Connell for a monster repeal demonstration planned for Sunday October 8th 1843. O'Connell however called the meeting off when he learned that the Castle authorities had banned it and that several regiments of troops were drawn up at Clontarf while the guns of the Pidgeon House Fort were trained on the appointed place of the assemblage.

DONNYCARNEY
CARNEY'S CHURCH

TRADITION HAS IT THAT SAINT PATRICK BUILT A CHURCH AT DONNYCARNEY WHICH IS SAID TO HAVE DISAPPEARED WITH THE COMING OF THE NORMANS.

IN THE TWELFTH CENTURY DERMOT McMURROUGH GRANTED TO THE PRIORY OF ALL HALLOWS THE LANDS OF DONNYCARNEY FROM WHICH THE MONKS DREW THEIR CHIEF SUPPLY OF GRAIN.

IN THE MID EIGHTEENTH CENTURY LORD CHARLEMONT ACQUIRED THE DONNYCARNEY LANDS AND CREATED A MAGNIFICENT ESTATE WHICH HE CALLED MARINO.

J.WREN '79.

Drumcondra

Drumcondraighe   (The Ridge of the Condraighe)

The name Drumcondra is derived from Drumcondraighe, or the Ridge of the Condraighe, a tribe who inhabited the area in the 2nd century. Drumcondra was originally a village in the townland of Clonturk, which is another ancient placename in this district. Since time immemorial a road or highway has cut through here to Drogheda. This was formerly known as the "Great Drogheda Road" and, in the 1450 Chancery Roll, it was called "The Royal Way".

During the middle ages the lands of Drumcondra were in the hands of monastic institutions and the monks farmed here until the 16th century suppression of the religious houses. The great north city abbey of St. Mary's maintained a home farm on the Drumcondra lands of Drishogue and Clonliffe, to supply their establishment with food.

For centuries the Priory of the Trinity (Christ Church) was in possession of the lands of Drumcondra, where the St. Joseph's Asylum for the male blind now stands. At the time of the dissolution these lands were leased to James Bathe, who had previously occupied Drimnagh Castle, and his son John built a castle here in 1560. After the death of John Bathe, in 1586, his widow married Sir William Warren, a soldier and a noted participant in the history of the Earl of Tyrone's rebellion.

On the afternoon of 3rd August 1591 a historic marriage took place in Drumcondra Castle. In the presence of a party of cavaliers, Mabel Bagenal of Turvey House, Co. Dublin, became the bride of Hugh O'Neill, 3rd Earl of Tyrone. Mabel Bagenal, whose brother Marshal Sir Henry Bagenal opposed the marriage, later libelled O'Neill saying he was already married. Thomas Jones, the bishop of Meath, she accused of solemnizing the nuptials of a bigamist. But these allegations were proved false. William Bathe, son of John Bathe, studied abroad and became a distinguished Jesuit. He accompanied the Papal Nuncio to Ireland in 1601.

After the Restoration in 1660, the castle and lands of Drumcondra were leased to Giles Martin. Seemingly he set up a brewing business here for his widow, in 1689, was in the possession of a brewery with seven horses. The castle's next occupant was Captain Chichester Phillips, who sat for Askeaton, Co. Limerick, in the Irish Parliament. It would appear that Drumcondra Castle had become ruinous by 1780, for in that year Sir Edward Newenham resided in a house on the site of the castle. The Carmelite Brothers opened the Asylum for the Male Blind here in 1882. Today it is under the care of the Rosminian Fathers.

The present Protestant church of St. John the Baptist at Drumcondra, which was dedicated in 1743, probably occupies the site of the Anglo-Norman church of Clonturk. The church was erected by Mary Coghill, the sister of local landlord Sir Marmaduke Coghill, whose memorial monument of Scheemakers stands within its walls.

In the adjoining graveyard lie the remains of the great architectural genius, the designer of Dublin's Custom House, James Gandon. He is interred in the same grave as Francis Grose, the antiquarian, who was his friend and fellow countryman. Other notable people buried at Drumcondra included Thomas Furlong the Wexford poet, Thomas Ryder the celebrated actor, and George Semple the Dublin architect whose works included St. Patrick's Hospital and Essex Bridge. In this century Patrick Heaney, who wrote the music of "The Soldiers Song", and local man Captain Seamus McGowan of the Irish Citizen Army, were buried at Drumcondra.

The oldest building in Drumcondra is Belvedere House, which is now St. Patrick's Teachers Training College and was built by Sir Robert Booth, a Chief Justice of the Kings Bench toward the end of the 17th century. A later owner of Belvedere House was Sir Marmaduke Coghill who, in 1725, built the splendid mansion, Drumcondra House. This now forms the central architectural feature of All Hallows College. The notorious Alderman John Claudius Beresford, who during the 1798 Insurrection tortured and flogged hundreds of suspected rebels, lived for some years at Drumcondra House. Today's bustling suburb of Drumcondra was in past centuries the home of local mill workers. The street names of Millbourne and Millmount Avenue recall this former industrial activity.

BLACKROCK

(Continued from Page 22)

Fort Lisle stood inside the gates of the present People's Park and, in 1793, became the Vauxhall gardens and amusement park.

Lisaniskean (Lios an Uisce), which came into the possession of Lady Arabella Denny in 1747 is also still in existence, as is Prospect, which later became St. Joseph's, a boarding school for the sons of the nobility and gentry.

Blackrock College was founded in 1860 by Father Jules Loman of the congregation of Holy Ghost fathers, when he arrived here from France and acquired the house and grounds of Castle Dawson, at Williamstown. Originally known as the French College, the late president Eamonn de Valera was its most distinguished pupil.

In the sporting field Blackrock College is long famous for its rugby sides but it is interesting to note that the local gaelic football club, the Feagh McHugh's, was supplied with most its players from the college in 1888, when it won the 2nd Dublin Football Championship.

In 1807 one of the greatest Irish sea tragedies occurred at Blackrock when two transports, the Prince of Wales packet and the Rochdale ran onto the rocks during a storm. One hundred and twenty soldiers were drowned in the Prince of Wales and another 265 passengers on the Rochdale lost their lives.

On December 17th 1834 the first train to run in Ireland passed through Blackrock on its journey from Westland Row to Dun Laoghaire. It was called the Hibernia. The last train ran on July 10th 1949.

DRUMCONDRA
THE RIDGE OF THE CONDRAIGHE

DRUMCONDRA CASTLE, THE SITE OF WHICH IS NOW OCCUPIED BY SAINT JOSEPHS HOME AND SCHOOL FOR THE BLIND WAS BUILT BY THE BATHE FAMILY IN TUDOR TIMES. IN THE CHAPEL ATTACHED TO THE CASTLE, HUGH O NEILL THE GREAT EARL OF TYRONE MARRIED MABEL BAGENAL IN AUGUST 1591 AND THE CELEBRATIONS LASTED FOR FIVE DAYS.

DRUMCONDRA CHURCH (C. OF. I.) BUILT IN 1743 CONTAINS THE GRAVE OF JAMES GANDON THE ARCHITECT OF THE CUSTOM HOUSE

DRUMCONDRA HOUSE NOW ALL HALLOWS COLLEGE WAS BUILT BY SIR MARMADUKE COGHILL IN THE EARLY PART OF THE EIGHTEENTH CENTURY

J. WREN 79

Dundrum

Dundrum

(The Fort on the Ridge)

Dundrum was originally part of the parish and townland of Taney, which took its name from Teach Nahi, the oratory of the Celtic saint Nahi. In early christian times Nahi's foundation became a major monastic centre with a resident bishop who presided over the neighbouring districts of Rathfarnham, Donnybrook and Kilgobbin.

After the Anglo-Norman invasion Taney was divided. Part of the lands, now called Churchtown, remained under ecclesiastical control while Dundrum became the fiefdom of the De Clahull family, one of whom, Sir John, was Marshal of the Lordship of Leinster in the 13th century. It was during this period that the first castle was built to ward off the Wicklow clans. It gave its name to the village that rose in its shadow. The lands later passed to the Baggot family and then the FitzWilliams, who restored the castle in 1596, during the revolt of O'Neill and O'Donnell.

In 1641 the castle was captured by insurgents and suffered severe damage in the wars of the period. In 1653 a Cromwellian officer, Lieutenant-Colonel Isaac Dobson occupied the castle and rennovated it. His son, Alderman Eliphal Dobson was the formost publisher of his day and printed the first Bible produced in Ireland. The castle passed to a series of tenants during the 18th century and had fallen into decay by the early 1800s. It still stands although the main building on the grounds is now a large 19th century residence built by Dr. Arthur Goff. Today it houses the offices of 'Southside Newspapers'.

In the 18th and early 19th century the Windy Arbour area of Dundrum was a favourite health resort of Dubliners. Here they came to drink goat's whey and the young Lord Cloncurry was one of the visitors.

Sir Thomas Lighton, Bart, a High Sheriff of County Dublin and former owner of Merville (now part of UCD, Belfield) was one of a number of distinguished citizens interred at Dundrum churchyard. Lighton began an adventurous career as a private soldier in the East India Company and saw much action in India. When he was captured by Tipoo Sahib, a leading protagonist of Sir Arthur Wellesley, the future Duke of Wellington, Lighton escaped disguised as a native. He subsequently brought his commanding officer's property back to England and received a reward of £20,000.

It was not until 1878 that Dundrum received its first Catholic parish church. Its three altars were built by Pearse and Sharpe, owned by James Pearse, father of Padraic and Willie, the 1916 leaders. By then Dundrum was a burgeoning suburb whose population had just reached 2,187. In the previous century it had less than a hundred dwellings, of which only nine "were of any consequence". The old church of St. Nahi had become the property of the Church of Ireland at the reformation. (Although the FitzWilliams had permitted the Catholic mass to be heard in Dundrum Castle for over 100 years afterwards.) But in 1818 St. Nahi's was replaced by Christ Church, which was consecrated on a site donated by Lord Pembroke, one of the major landlords in the district.

The reason for the expansion of Dundrum - and many other suburbs - was the advent of the railways. The opening of the Harcourt Street to Shankill line, via Dundrum could take passengers from the city centre to Dundrum in 16 minutes. It was closed down in 1959.

An old water fountain stands in the Main Street, near the site of the old railway station and was erected to commemorate the death of Dr. Isaac Usher. He was killed when a car reversed over him in the station yard in 1917. He lived in Laurel Lodge, where the housing estate of Laurel Drive and Laurel Road now stands.

The Irish industrial revival in the early 1900s left its mark on Dundrum with the establishment, on Sandyford Road, of the Dun Emer Guild, at the house of the same name. Amongst the founders of the Guild, which produced embroidered works such as tapestries and carpets, were two daughters of John B. Yeats who had trained under the famous designer, William Morris, at his works in Merton Abbey. The Cuala press was also established as a result of their efforts locally. Of more longterm importance as an employer was the establishment of the Pye Ireland in 1930 at Temple Lane at the centre of the village.

The present owner of the 13th century Dundrum Castle, architect David Johnston, hopes to restore the roofless building within the next decade. Conversion however will not begin until archaeological excavation is completed. Finds so far in the dig have included pottery and bronze artefacts and a human skull with a sawn off cranium. Also found were a unique moat and drawbridge system which are still being excavated.

Dundrum's most famous son, Stephen Roche from Meadowmount, made sporting history last year. The 27 year old Dubliner was the first man to ever win the Giro d'Italia, Tour de France and World Cycling Championship in one year.

DUNDRUM

SAINT NATHI FOUNDED A CHURCH AT DUNDRUM IN THE 6TH OR 7TH CENTURY AND GAVE THE NAME TO THE ANCIENT DEANERY OF TANEY (TEACH NATHI). FOR A LONG PERIOD TANEY WAS A GREAT ECCLESIASTICAL CENTRE.

EARLY IN THE LAST CENTURY MANY INVALIDS CAME TO DUNDRUM TO DRINK MOUNTAIN GOAT'S MILK.

DUNDRUM CASTLE NOW AN IVY CLAD RUIN WAS IN OCTOBER 1641 TAKEN BY INSURGENTS WHO HELD OUT FOR SEVERAL MONTHS.

J WREN

Dun Laoghaire

Dun Laoghaire

(Laoghaire's Fort)

Despite its ancient name Dun Laoghaire is essentially a modern town, owing its creation to the dilapidated state of Dublin port in the early nineteenth century and the British admiralty's need for a secure steel packet port near to the British mainland.

The town's name comes from a fifth century fort built by Laoghaire, King of Tara, whose chief claim to fame was his conversion to Christianity by St. Patrick. The ruins of the fort survived until the 1800s, when a martello tower was built on the site. The tower and the older fort were demolished in 1836 to make way for an extension of the railway link with Dublin. The debris was used to fill in the old harbour. It is covered today by the old coalyards and the Albright and Wilson works.

During the middle ages Dun Laoghaire was nothing more than a sleepy fishing village offering a haven for ships awaiting entry to Dublin or Dalkey harbours. The most notable event in its history was the landing of the Earl of Essex as Viceroy in 1672.

The eighteenth century saw Dun Laoghaire grow in popularity as a bathing spa and it appears on Thomas Burgh's map of 1728. A coffee house was built some years later to cater for travellers disembarking from ships on their way to Dublin. Like the martello tower, it was demolished to make way for the railways in the 1830s.

A new pier was erected between 1755 and 1767, financed by a grant from the Irish House of Commons, to handle the extra shipping. It became known as the dry pier, because it rapidly silted up.

The 1770s saw the beginning of the South Wales coal trade, one of the chief industries at Dun Laoghaire over the next 200 years. On July 19th, 1785, the Dun Laoghaire barge carried out one of the most unusual sea rescues in Irish history, when it picked up Richard Crosbie, Ireland's first aeronaut, when his balloon landed near the harbour after a successful flight from Leinster lawn.

Early in the nineteenth century Captain William Bligh (the former captain of the Bounty) was sent to survey Dublin bay by the Admiralty. Bligh found Dun Laoghaire harbour "had little to recommend it". Nevertheless, several martello towers were erected during the invasion scares caused by the Napoleonic wars and George's Street developed along the pathway between them.

Ships increasingly used the port because of the shifting sandbars, which made direct approaches to the Dublin quays dangerous. It was the tragic loss of two ships in 1807, the HMS Prince of Wales and the Rochdale troop transport with 380 men on board, which forced the government to consider Dun Laoghaire as a new port. A petition of the local nobility and gentry in 1808 demanded an "asylum harbour" in the area, even though work had already begun on Howth as a steam packet connection with Britain.

Eventually work was begun on Dun Laoghaire in 1817, after much lobbying by Captain Toutcher and other local men of substance. Toutcher also persuaded landowners on Killiney Hill and the Hill of Dalkey to allow granite to be quarried free of charge from their lands for the harbour.

The actual work was done under the direction of John Rennie. Between 1817 and 1821 the main east and west piers were constructed, encompassing 250 acres of water. Labourers employed on the work settled mainly on Dalkey commons, but this period also saw the birth of the squalid slums at Glasthule and York Street, which were not cleared until the turn of the century. Wages for the workmen on the harbour were ten shillings (50p) a week.

It took another 30 years to complete the harbour with the addition of a magnificent granite battery on the east pier, one of the world's first anenometers (to measure wind force), two light houses to mark the entrance to the port and a coastguard station. Fortunately all of these fine buildings are still standing.

The final mark of approval for Dun Laoghaire came with the visit of King George IV in 1821, when the burgeoning township changed its name to Kingstown. A hideous obelisk was erected on the spot where the monarch embarked for England.

In marked contrast is the absence of even a plaque to commemorate 20,000 soldiers who left from the then new Victoria wharf in 1854 to fight in the Crimea, few returned. Now incorporated in the Carlisle pier at the centre of the

ferryport. This wharf has probably witnessed the departure of more emigrants than any other spot in Ireland. The same pier saw the arrival of thousands of troops from England to crush the Rising in April 1916.

The completion of Ireland's first commuter railway, linking Dun Laoghaire with Dublin, five-and-a-half miles away ensured the port's continued viability. In 1836 an imposing station was built to a design by J. S. Mulvany. The actual railway track was built on a submerged line so as not to spoil the view for Dun Laoghaire's new residents. Mulvany also designed the Royal St. George Yacht Club clubhouse overlooking the harbour, some seven years later.

In 1826 the steam packet service was transferred from Howth to Kingstown, as it was now known and rapidly grew to be the largest urban centre in Ireland after Dublin, Belfast and Cork. In 1834 it was given its own town commission, but it was not until 1930 that the outlying suburbs of Dalkey, Blackrock and Ballybrack were brought together in the new borough of Dun Laoghaire. (The town reverted to its old Irish name in 1920, during the War of Independence.)

This did not prevent the construction of the Town Hall in 1880 on a palatial scale. The architect was J. L. Robinson, the builder was Michael Meade and the building was undoubtedly the most imposing ever constructed in the town. Its venetian palace design, with circular piered balconies and windows are highlighted by the use of different coloured stone. The original design had been in brick but the city fathers decided they could afford stone. The final cost was double the original estimate of £8,000. The Town Hall tower is 120 feet high.

The nineteenth century saw the construction of no less than 12 churches in Dun Laoghaire. The fact that only three of them were catholic underlines the essential ascendency character of the town. Well worth a visit is the Mariners church at Haigh terrace, built by the Church of Ireland in 1836. It now houses the National Maritime Museum.

The only building of any antiquity in Dun Laoghaire, Corrig Castle (off Tivoli Road) was demolished in 1945. Corrig House was built nearby in 1815. Its driveway later became Corrig Avenue

(Continued on Page 98)

DUN LAOGHAIRE

DUN LAOGHAIRE WAS THE FIFTH CENTURY COASTAL FORT OF KING LAOGHAIRE OF TARA.

THE ARTIFICIAL HARBOUR OF DUN LAOGHAIRE WAS DESIGNED BY THE MOST OUTSTANDING BRITISH ENGINEER OF HIS TIME JOHN RENNIE

KINGSTOWN HARBOUR 1834

JOHN RENNIE 1761 — 1821

NATIONAL MARITIME MUSEUM FORMELY EPISCOPAL MARINERS CHURCH, KINGSTOWN

THE PAVILION ERECTED IN 1903 AND BURNED DOWN IN 1915.

Finglas

Fionn Glas

(The Clear Stream)

Finglas, or Fionn Glas meaning the clear stream, derives its name from a streamlet which flows through this area and merges with the river Tolka at Finglas Bridge. From the early Irish sagas we learn that Conn of the hundred battles attacked the rebellious Fianna at Finglas and finally defeated them at nearby Castleknock.

The Abbey of Finglas, an early Christian mission in Fingal was founded about 560 A.D. by Saint Canice of Cianach, a member of the sept of the Ciannachta who ruled north Dublin in Celtic times. Canice, who attended the famous school of Saint Mobhi at Glasnevin alongside such distinguished fellow students as Columcille, Comgall and Ciaran, was possibly a native of this place and chose the beautiful sylvan setting of Finglas as the site of his first foundation.

The Abbey of Finglas grew in importance and flourished for centuries. Along with the Monastery of Tallaght it became known as the "Two Eyes of Ireland" and, although there is no record of activities at Finglas, there is a long list of abbots and bishops associated with the establishment.

A link with the original church of Canice at Finglas is the ancient granite cross of Nethercross which now stands beside the entrance gate to the old village burial ground. The cross which stood for twelve centuries in the abbey grounds was taken down and buried in 1649 to avoid desecration by the Cromwellian soldiery. The old cross remained buried and almost forgotten until 1806 when the Rev. Robert Walsh, the Vicar of Finglas, discovered its hiding place and had it re-erected in the ancient graveyard.

Austin Cooper in his diary of 1799 mentions however having seen the cross at that time, which brings into dispute the story that the cross was buried during the penal times. There was a Viking raid at Finglas in 795 and the church of Saint Canice was plundered and burned, the nave of the present ruined church dates from the 11th or 12th century and is built in the Romanesque style.

During the summer of 1171 an Irish army of several thousand men under the command of high king Rory O'Connor of Connaught encamped at Finglas and besieged the city of Dublin. After being cut off and surrounded for two months a small Anglo-Norman force led by Milo De Cogan made a desperate sally against the Irish at Finglas and, taking them completely by surprise, routed them.

Some 12th century weapons found at a quarry at Finglaswood in the last century were said to have been left behind by the fleeing clansmen. Some months later, at Christmas 1171, Henry II came to Ireland after the murder of Thomas A Beckett and garrisoned a large force of archers at Finglas.

Geraldus, the Welsh chronicler, relates how the sacred yews planted by Saint Canice himself at Finglas were cut down by the archers for the making of arrows and were burned by the Norman soldiers. This deed brought upon them divine displeasure and they perished as result of pestilence.

During Anglo-Norman times, with the exception of Swords, Finglas became the most valuable of the manors of the archbishops of Dublin. In 1228 archbishop Luke built an episcopal residence here and his successor Fulk De Sandford died at Finglas. The building which was called the "Court" was afterwards the property of Archbishop Ussher and its site is today represented by the georgian dwelling "Fort William". This is now used by the Sisters of the Holy Faith.

Finglas was an important part of the Norman Pale and was raided and pillaged on many occasions by the mountain septs of the O'Byrnes and the O'Tooles. Some distance to the north of Finglas village stands Dunsoghley castle which was built by Thomas Plunkett, Chief Justice of the Kings Bench in the early 15th century. The building is a fine rectangular tower which retains the original oak roof trusses.

When rebellion broke out in 1641 the house of Colonel Arthur Hill at Finglas was captured by Luke Netterville and his followers and the lead from the roof was used to make bullets. Shortly after this they came under attack by crown forces in vastly superior numbers and, after a stubborn resistence, the insurgents were finally forced to disperse. In 1649 the Duke of Ormond camped his army at Finglas for a month before the battle of Rathmines and 41 years later William of Orange also camped his forces at Finglas after his victory on the Boyne.

In the 17th and 18th centuries Finglas was famous for its May Day festivities when the Maypole, bedecked with multi-coloured ribbons, stood in the village centre. Here, on May Day, came Dubliners in their hundreds to take part in the many novel sports and activities. These events included ass races, sack races, hunts after pigs with shaven tails, blind fold chases after a bell ringer, and athletic contests of all kinds.

The great annual fun fair of gaiety and mirth gradually degenerated into a rowdy affair and eventually went the way of the notorious Donnybrook Fair. In 1841 when the reforming Father Henry Young was appointed to the parish he condemned the sports as pagan and called the Maypole the "Devil's Potstick". In 1843 he had it felled, putting a final halt to the high jinks at Finglas.

FINGLAS
THE CLEAR STREAM

FOR CENTURIES FINGLAS WAS FAMOUS FOR ITS MAYDAY FESTIVITIES WHERE DUBLINERS DANCED AROUND THE MAY-POLE AND MADE MERRY.

LEGEND HAS IT THAT ST. PATRICK BLESSED THE HOLY WELL AT FINGLAS WHEN HE VISITED THE DISTRICT DURING HIS TRAVELS.

THE ONLY REMAINING LINK WITH THE ABBEY OF FINGLAS IS THE ANCIENT STONE CROSS WHICH STANDS IN THE OLD CEMETARY.

J. WREN '79

Glasnevin

The district of Glasnevin, through which the river Tolka courses, was in Celtic times called Glas Naeidhe, or Naeidhe's stream after a local chieftain.

It is believed that the Protestant church at Glasnevin occupies part of the site of an ancient monastery founded here in the 6th century. Saint Mobhi, who was also known as Berchan Clairinech, the flat faced, or crippled, established a seat of learning on the banks of the Tolka at Glasnevin, which preceded that at Finglas.

Among the many ecclesiastics who went to study under Mobhi were Saint Columba and Saint Canice. The latter founded Finglas. An ancient legend recalls that during Columba's sojourn at Glasnevin he miraculously transferred the students cells from the south to the north bank of the Tolka one winter's evening. After Saint Mobhi's death in 544, as a result of plague, his successors as abbots at Glasnevin included Cialtrog, who died in 741, Elphin, who died in 753 and Maoltuile, who died in 882.

After the Norman invasion the church and lands of Glasnevin became the property of the prior of the Holy Trinity (Christ Church Cathedral). The lands at Glasnevin were farmed by the priory and, in 1326 there were 28 tenants, including Sir David the Chaplain, Nicholas the Clerk, Hugh the Smith, Yvor the Turner and Maurice the driver. In the 15th century increasing numbers of leases were granted on the church land. Nicholas Barrett held a great meadow near the Tolka and Geoffrey Fox owned much local land and livestock. Details of the goods left to Fox by his two wives survive in the deeds of Christchurch. In the case of his second wife, Agnes Lawless, they included a mazer, six silver spoons, linen cloth and a great store of bacon.

In 1542 the villagers of Glasnevin participated in the cruel sport of bull baiting and a bull ring stood in the village centre. Glasnevin also had an unsavoury reputation for thieves, robbers and loose living. In 1725 Dr. King, the Protestant archbishop of Dublin, stated that when any couple had a mind to be wicked they would retire to the harbour of Glasnevin.

The village was also used as a base for rebel operations during the wars of the Confederation. In 1642 a rebel force under Colonel Hugh Byrne spent some time encamped at Glasnevin, from whence a night raid was made on Oxmanstown.

At the beginning of the 18th century Sir John Rogerson, the merchant and ship-owner after whom the well known quay is named, came to reside at Glasnevin. Rogerson's residence, which was called Glasnevin house, now forms part of the Holy Faith convent. Henry Mitchel, a wealthy banker, later acquired Glasnevin house and laid the gardens before he died in 1768. In the early 19th century Glasnevin house and the surrounding lands were acquired by the Rt. Rev. Charles Lindsay, the Protestant bishop of Kildare, after whom Lindsay Road takes its name. The lands were eventually sold by Bishop Lindsay's heirs to the Holy Faith nuns – also included were part of the present cemetery grounds.

The beautiful National Botanical Gardens at Glasnevin date from 1795, when they were laid out by Doctor Walter Wade, professor of botany to the Dublin Society. The gardens are on land which was originally the property of Thomas Tickell, the poet biographer of Addison. Tickell settled in Ireland in 1724. Addison, who died in 1719 some years before Tickell acquired the Glasnevin property, has a walk named after him in the mistaken belief that the great essayist walked these grounds.

The Botanic Gardens came under state control in 1878 and is a favourite retreat of Dubliners and visitors. Many rare plants are displayed in the greenhouses and the rose gardens are particularly lovely. There are many fine tree specimens here and near the main entrance is the Thomas Moore rose which was raised from a cutting from the flower which inspired "The Last Rose of Summer".

The Bon Secours hospital occupies the site of Delville, the eighteenth century home of Dr. Patrick Delaney, Chancellor of Saint Patrick's Cathedral and his wife Mary. Dr. Delaney, an intimate friend of Dean Swift, had his gardens laid out in the Dutch manner and spent money lavishly on his Glasnevin estate. When his first wife died he married Mrs. Mary Pendarves (nee Granville), the widow of a Cornish Squire. she was an accomplished letter writer and her correspondence vividly captured the lifestyles of ascendency classes, though the plight of the native poor is rarely mentioned. At Delville the Delaneys entertained the nobility of the day lavishly and Lord and Lady Chesterfield were among those received here.

Swift was a regular visitor to Delville and after his famous Drapiers Letters were published, went into hiding in an outhouse where, it is reputed, a printing press was installed. Another building associated with the Dean of St. Patrick's was the unusual Ink Bottle School. The School was designed by Swift and built to resemble an ink bottle. It stood at the top of Botanic Avenue and was demolished in 1901. Delville suffered the same fate.

The great cemetery at Glasnevin was opened in February 1832 and was the successful outcome of years of agitation led by Daniel O'Connell for adequate burial facilities in the city. Originally called Prospect cemetery, the country's greatest patriots were laid to rest here. Daniel O'Connell himself lies in a vault beneath a 160 foot high replica of an Irish round tower made from white granite. Among the many fine monuments is the beautiful memorial to those who fell in 1916, the great granite slab which commemorates Parnell and the lifesize figure which stands over the grave of Barry Sullivan representing him in his most famous role of Hamlet.

The Protestant church of St. Mobhi, beside which stand some old world cottages at Church Avenue, was rebuilt in 1707 by Sir John Rogerson and incorporated a square tower of an earlier date. In 1830 the peace of the little village was shattered by the blast of gunshot as a pitched battle took place in Saint Mobhi's churchyard between graverobbers and a party of watchers who came upon them.

The modern church of Our Lady of Dolours, at Glasnevin Bridge, replaces an old wooden chapel which was erected here in 1881 and housed the altar and tabernacle originally used in Newgate prison, Green Street, Dublin. The new church was opened by Archbishop Dermot Ryan on March 19th, 1972 and is a remarkable example of modern church architecture. Shaped like a pyramid, it was designed by Vincent Gallagher and Associates.

Another striking new building is the headquarters of the Meteorological Service, which stands on Glasnevin Hill. Again it is pyramidal in shape and was designed thus to avoid light being blotted out from low rise buildings on adjoining land. These include the headquarters of the Institute for Industrial Research and Standards. The Meteorological Service

(Continued on Page 58)

In the sixth century Saint Mobhi founded a monastery on the banks of the Tolka at Glasnevin.

GLASNEVIN
NAEIDHE'S STREAM

O'Connell Monument Glasnevin Cemetery

Burial place of Daniel O'Connell

INK BOTTLE SCHOOL

GLASNEVIN

Mrs. Delaney, remarkable 18th century letter writer, who lived with her husband Doctor Delaney at Delville, Glasnevin.

Great Palm House Botanic Gardens, Glasnevin

J.WREN

Howth (Hoved)

Binn Eadhair   (Eadhair's Hill)

The scenic grandeur of this rocky promontary situated nine and a half miles north-east of Dublin city has thrilled both Dubliner and visitor alike for centuries past. On a clear day the mountains of Wales can be seen from the summit of this peninsural hill, its volcanic rock being the oldest in Ireland.

The hill is rich in legendary and historic associations, for here according to tradition the people of Parthalon lived at the dawn of Irish history. Crimthan, an Irish king, who reigned during the early Christian era, had his fortress eyrie on the site of the present Baily lighthouse and from there he made many forays into Roman Britain bringing back slaves and booty.

According to the saga of Fionn and the Fianna, Howth was one of their military stations and a watch tower was erected there as a look out for approaching enemy ships. A dolmen in the grounds of Howth Castle is said to be the burial place of Aideen who died of grief when she learned of the death of her husband, Oscar who was killed at the battle of Gabra in 248 A.D.

The Viking invaders of the 9th and 10th centuries made Howth one of their strongholds and the Danish survivors of the field of Clontarf fled here in 1014 and escaped in the longships of their countrymen. The defeated Norsemen returned however to Howth, for the Irish annals record two 11th century battles here between the Irish and the Norsemen.

With the coming of the Normans in the 12th century, the manor of Howth was granted by Henry II to Sir Almeric Tristram, one of the invading knights. To commemorate a fierce battle which was fought on the north side of the hill between the Norman force and the Danish occupiers on St. Lawrence's Day, Sir Almeric adopted that saint's name, which remained the family name thereafter.

The sword with which Sir Almeric fought on that day is now preserved in Howth Castle and a St. Lawrence Day was held in Howth until about 1830. The first St. Lawrence stronghold built by Sir Almeric was a wooden structure which was situated where the Martello Tower now stands on a hill to the east of the town.

The present Howth Castle stands on the site of an earlier one and was rebuilt by the 20th Earl in 1564. It consists of an embattled range flanked by towers and was formerly surrounded by a moat. In the 18th century further improvements were made and its interior is rich in antiques and paintings including a portrait of Dean Swift by Bindon.

A prominent figure in Irish history associated with Howth is Grace O'Malley, the Western Sea Queen. According to the story, Grace O'Malley (also known as Grainuaile) returning from a visit to Queen Elizabeth of England had to seek shelter during a storm at Howth. On approaching Howth Castle she became highly indignant when she discovered the gates closed during dinner time and considered this a breach of the custom of Irish hospitality. Seizing the young heir to Lord Howth she carried him away to her castle in Co. Mayo where she held him prisoner until she received a written pledge from his father that the gates would never be shut again at dinner hour.

The St. Lawrences were one of the leading families of the Pale for centuries and their lands stretched from Howth to Killester. They also held tracts of land in the North County Dublin. During the Geraldine Rebellion of 1543, John Allen, the Archbishop of Dublin was dragged from his bed at Artane Castle where he had sought the shelter of his friend, Thomas Howth, alias St. Lawrence, ward to the heir of that place and was murdered. During this Rebellion Lord Thomas Fitzgerald placed artillary on Howth Hill and from that strategic height cannonaded the English troop vessels in the waters below.

On the death of the 30th Baron of Howth his property, due to failure of a male heir, passed Mr. Julian Faisford St. Lawrence of Offington, Sussex, his nephew.

One of the most important relics of Howth's mediaeval period consists of the ruins of the Collegiate Parish Church of the Blessed Virgin Mary ("Saint Mary's Abbey"). This was founded in 1235 and is now a national monument. The remains consist of a 13th century nave and chancel with the ruins of 15th century college or priest's residence lying to the south of the church.

Howth harbour was built between 1807 and 1814, replacing Ringsend as the venue for the Holyhead mail packet service but it was not a success. The station was removed to Dun Laoghaire in 1836.

On 26th July 1914 the harbour was the scene of the Howth gun running when 900 rifles were landed from Erskine Childers's yacht, the Asgard, to the awaiting Irish Volunteers under the command of Cathal Brugha.

One mile from the harbour lies the rocky islet of Ireland's Eye on which stands the ruins of St. Nessan's Church which dates from 1844. It was restored on the site of the early christian monastery of the Sons of Nessan. An ancient illuminated gospel book the Garland of Howth was once a prize possession here and is now in Trinity College, Dublin.

AIDEEN'S GRAVE, HOWTH

HOWTH
NORSE - HOVUD - HEAD

THIS ROCKY PROMONTARY 9½ MILES N.E. OF DUBLIN RENOWNED FOR ITS — MAGNIFICENT SCENERY IS RICH IN STORY & LEGEND. ACCORDING TO THE SAGA OF FINN & THE FIANNA A WATCH TOWER STOOD ON THE TOP OF BEANN EADAIR (EADARS PEAK), THE NAME BY WHICH HOWTH WAS KNOWN DURING CELTIC TIMES, FROM WHICH APPROACHING ENEMY SHIPS COULD BE OBSERVED.

HOWTH CASTLE, THE SEAT OF THE ST. LAWRENCE FAMILY FOR CENTURIES, HAS ASSOCIATIONS WITH THE WESTERN SEA-QUEEN, GRACE O MALLEY. THERE IS A STORY THAT GRANUAILE AS SHE WAS KNOWN, KIDNAPPED THE YOUNG HEIR TO THE EARL OF HOWTH BECAUSE THE CASTLE GATES WERE CLOSED TO HER WHEN SHE SOUGHT SHELTER THERE.

ON JULY 26TH 1914 A CARGO OF 900 RIFLES WERE LANDED AT HOWTH HARBOUR FROM ERSKINE CHILDERS YACHT, THE ASGARD, TO THE AWAITING IRISH VOLUNTEERS.

Page 55

Inchicore and Kilmainham

Inchicore or Guaire's river meadow is another example of Dublin nomenclature commemorating a forgotten chieftain of the celtic period. Or, as is not uncommon it may also be interpreted as an Irish placename, Inis Coar, the Island of the Berries.

The area originally formed the western portion of the lands of Kilmainham, on which St. Mhighneann founded a monastery in the seventh century. When the Vikings founded Dublin in the ninth century they built a series of "garths" and villages at sites along the ridge from the present site of Dublin castle and Christchurch to Kilmainham, Islandbridge, Inchicore and Clondalkin.

In 1866, while gravel was being drawn from the sloping ground near the present Con Colbert Road, corporation workmen found several skeletons with an accumulation of Norse household articles and arms. At nearby Kilmainham more Norse specimens were found in the last century when a railway cutting was being excavated and in 1933 many viking interments and weapons were discovered when the War Memorial gardens at Islandbridge were laid out.

In 1014 Brian Boru set up his headquarters at Kilmainham and the encampment probably included part of Inchicore. After the anglo-norman invasion the lands of Kilmainham were granted by Stronbow to the military order of the Knights of St. John of Jerusalem, also known as the Knights Hospitallers. The order held land in many counties and when their rival military order, the Knights Templar were suppressed in 1308 their lands at Clontarf were awarded to the hospitallers.

The Norman magnate, Hugh Tyrell of Castleknock, presented the Priory of Kilmainham with lands which included Islandbridge and much of the present Phoenix Park. When the Duke of Ormond opened in the Phoenix Park in the late seventeenth century, Inchicore, Kilmainham and Islandbridge were originally enclosed within it for some 20 years.

Inchicore was apparently thickly wooded in early times and there was a 41 acre wood there at the dissolution of the monasteries in 1541. The Priory had a fulling mill on the Camac river and 30 acres of pasture on the south side of Golden Bridge.

Before the rebellion of 1641 a substantial brick residence had been built at Inchicore. In Sir William Petty's famous survey of Ireland under Cromwell, he found a population of only three English and five Irish in 1659. The townland of Inchicore West, which includes the modern dualcarriageway at Bothar Coilbeard had five landowners, all Irish papists. They were Arthur Malone of Lismolin, White, Pierce and Shelton of Dublin, and Fagan of Feltrim.

Inchicore house was built by Arthur Annesley, the fourth Lord Altham in the early eighteenth century. The house, which was demolished 20 years ago, stood on the ridge overlooking the Liffey close to the present Pine Tree public house on Sarsfield Road. Lord Altham made many additions to his three storey redbrick residence before his death in 1727. His son and heir, James Annesley, was the subject of a most remarkable succession case.

James Annesley was born in 1715 at Wexford shortly before his father separated from his English wife and became involved with a Miss Gregory. Lord Altham planned to marry his mistress as soon as his wife, who was ailing, died. The domineering Miss Gregory persuaded Lord Altham to board out his son to a woman in Ship Street and he was left to roam the streets as a vagabond until he was befriended and sheltered by a linen draper called Dominick Farrell. After Lord Altham's death his title was assumed by his brother Richard Annesley, who had young James deported to Philadelphia as an indentured servant, little better than a slave.

After much hardship and adventures in the new world, James Annesley obtained his freedom and was shipped to England when he was 25. While in England he accidentally shot a man at Staines and his uncle, now officially recognising his nephew as the fifth Lord Altham made every effort to have him indicted for murder. James Annesley was however acquitted and instituted proceedings to obtain his inheritance. In a 15-day hearing, the longest court case till then in Irish legal history, James Annesley succeeded in his claim. However, his uncle obtained a writ of error and the case was still unsettled when James Annesley died as a result of his hardships in 1760.

During the court proceedings there were frequent references to Lord Altham's house at Inchicore and to a nearby inn called the Butcher's Arms, which gave its name to the local townland. The site of the inn is now occupied by the De La Salle Brothers school in Ballyfermot.

Goldenbridge, which spans the Camac river at Inchicore and gives its name to the adjoining townland was known four hundred years ago as Glydon Bridge. At that time a Richard Rawson had a cloth fulling mill there and by the late 18th century Golden Bridge had flour, paper and barley mills.

The old Spa Road tramworks at Goldenbridge derives its name from two mineral springs discovered here in 1813. The Waterloo Spa, named after Wellington's great vistory of the same year, attracted immense crowds because of the curative properties attributed to its waters. The Golden Bridge convent girls' school now occupies the site. The Richmond Spa was at the rear of the present Spa Road factory and was also popular.

Richmond infantry barracks was built about 1807 and named after the then Lord Lieutenant, the Duke of Richmond who held the post from 1807 to 1813. Following the withdrawal of the British forces in 1922 the Free State army took over the barracks, which were renamed after Commandant General Tom Keogh, killed in the Civil War.

In 1916 six of the seven signatories of the Proclamation were held with many other rebel prisoners in the barrack's gymnasium. The republican prisoners included Patrick and William Pearse, Thomas Clarke, Sean McDermott, Thomas McDonagh, Eamonn Ceannt, the Plunkett brothers Joseph and George, Eamon de Valera, Michael Collins, T. W. Cosgrave, Major Sean MacBride, Countess Markiewicz, Arthur Griffith, Noel Lemass and Thomas Ashe.

In 1924 Keogh barracks was converted into Corporation dwellings and in 1969 Keogh Square, as it was then called, was demolished to make way for the present flats complex of St. Michael's estate. Today the only remnants of the barracks is the old gymnasium, owned by the Christian Brothers and Saint Michael's catholic church which had been the garrison church. The Bulfin Road housing estate stands on the site of the old parade ground.

In 1829, the year of catholic emancipation, the first catholic cemetery to be opened since the dissolution of the monasteries, was solemnly blessed at Goldenbridge. It was the principal

(Continued on Page 58)

INCHICORE

AFTER THE 1916 RISING MANY OF THE ARRESTED REBELS WERE HELD IN RICHMOND BARRACKS, INCHICORE. AMONG THEM WERE THE PLUNKETT BROTHERS, JOHN, JOSEPH AND GEORGE (SHOWN IN UNIFORM BELOW)

COUNCILLOR W.P. PARTRIDGE

THE ALL-IRELAND HURLING AND FOOTBALL FINALS OF 1889

EARLY IN THE NINETEENTH CENTURY THE SPA AT INCHICORE WAS A POPULAR RENDEZVOUS.

WERE PLAYED AT INCHICORE

J.WREN

Inchicore and Kilmainham

(Continued from Page 56)

catholic cemetery in the city until Glasnevin was opened in 1832. Amongst those interred there was W. T. Cosgrave, first president of the Irish Free State. The Mercy nuns from Baggot Street came to Goldenbridge in 1855 and opened a convent school for girls there.

The Oblate fathers arrived at Inchicore in 1856 and with the help of workers from the nearby Great Southern and Western Railway works erected a temporary wooden chapel in four days. This was replaced by the present splendid church of Mary Immaculate in 1878.

The railway works are today the main engineering centre for CIE and until the late 1970s buses were also built at the nearby Spa Road works. However this was privatised and the Spa Road factory, run by the Belgian company Van Hool, quickly closed and no buses or coaches are made today in Dublin.

A number of political meetings were held in the Inchicore area during the last two decades of the last century. The first was by Home Rulers outside Kilmainham jail in 1888 and was addressed by Willie Redmond MP, W. J. Clancy MP and many others. On Sunday 7th June, 1891, Charles Stewart Parnell visited Inchicore house, the home of one of the staunchest supporters Edward Holohan, the chairman of the Kilmainham commissioners. In the grounds of the house the clearly ailing leader showed signs of physical deterioration but spoke to over 10,000. Twelve bands played at the meeting where the crowd's response visibly uplifted Parnell's spirits.

Inchicore holds an important place in Dublin GAA history for it was here that Dublin won its first all-Ireland hurling title (1889) when the hurling and football finals were played in the village. The Dublin Kickham's selection defeated a Clare (Tulla) side which had decided to play barefoot because of the soaked state of the ground.

The exact location is not certain but P. J. Kavanagh in the Irish Press GAA Golden Jubilee supplement of 1934 said it took place "at the back of the present range of houses some yards below Inchicore church". This claim and local tradition point to the present Tyrconnell Park housing estate as the site of these early all-Irelands.

William Partridge, the Sligo born trade union leader established a united workers council at the Inchicore railway works and led a strike there in 1902. In 1913 Partridge, then a Labour councillor, was leader of the local ITGWU branch in the 1913 lock-out. As a member of the Citizen Army he fought at the College of Surgeons in 1916 and was given ten years penal servitude. Due to ill-health he was released and died soon afterwards.

James Standish O'Grady, the Irish literary revivalist and historian lived in Inchicore at 3 Madeline Terrace. In his younger days James Joyce was a frequent visitor and refers to the district in the 'After the Race' story in Dubliners. There are also references to it in 'Ulysses' and 'Finnegan's Wake'.

Glasnevin

(Continued from Page 52

building was designed by Derry architect Liam McCormack. It stands on the site of Marlboro house, a former detention centre for boys in trouble with the law.

An unusual feature of Glasnevin is that many street names date to the 18th and early 19th centuries. For instance Botanic Avenue was once called Corry's Lane or Codey's Lane, after James Corry, a linen merchant and local resident in the 18th century. Lindsay Road and Crawford Avenue, we are told, were called after the Bishop of Kildare, the Rt. rev. Charles Lindsay, who was also a son of the Earl of crawford. The Crawford family lived in the area for many years and Carlingford Road also derives its name from one of their local residences, Carlingford house.

Following the example of the Dalkey School Project and the Bray School Project the North Dublin National School Project was established in 1983 in the old school house of the 'Model National School' at Church Avenue. The school is run on four fundamental and inter-related principles i.e. that the school should be multi-denominational, co-educational, child centered and democratically run. The school now has 8 classrooms and is considered a huge success. The principal of the school is Ms Sally Shiels.

Castleknock

(Continued from Page 26)

Thomas Troy, Catholic Archbishop of Dublin was born here.

There was a general revival of trade and agriculture in the 17th century, with the Cromwellian, Colonel Richard Lawrence, establishing a linen industry in nearby Chapelizod. John Sweetman, one of the famous Sweetman family once described as the richest commoners in Ireland, settled at Abbotstown. Huntstown, Dunsink, Cappoge, Blanchardstown and other townlands of the parish began to assume their own identities at this time and each was dominated by its own great landowning family. Perhaps the best known of these were the Rowles's who gave their name to Rowlestown and represented the area in several parliaments.

It is the beautiful scenery of the Liffey valley and the Phoenix Park which make Castleknock such a high amenity area today and one in much demand. The ruins of the castle are the only reminder of its past glory and lie in the grounds behind St Vincent's College, which was established here in 1834.

In 1184 Richard Tyrell, in honour of St Brigid, gave lands at Clonsillaw to endow a small abbey following the rules of St Augustine. In 1219 it came under the priory of Little Malvern in Worcestershire, a convent of the Benedictines and the ownership of local ecclesiastical prebends and tithes were a matter of bitter dispute for several centuries. Traditionally the local church has always been named after St Brigid and the present Church of Ireland building, is a fine and early example of the Gothic revival style in ecclesiastical architecture.

KILMAINHAM
CHURCH OF MHAIGHNEANN

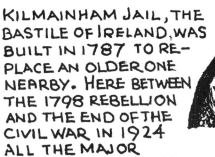

KILMAINHAM JAIL, THE BASTILE OF IRELAND, WAS BUILT IN 1787 TO REPLACE AN OLDER ONE NEARBY. HERE BETWEEN THE 1798 REBELLION AND THE END OF THE CIVIL WAR IN 1924 ALL THE MAJOR POLITICAL PRISONERS WERE HELD.

THE SEVEN SIGNATORIES OF THE 1916 PROCLAMATION AND MOST OF THE OTHER LEADERS OF THE EASTER RISING WERE EXECUTED IN THE STONE BREAKING YARD AT KILMAINHAM BY FIRING SQUAD.

P.H. PEARSE

THOMAS J. CLARKE

JAMES CONNOLLY

THOMAS MAC DONAGH

EAMONN CEANNT

JOSEPH PLUNKETT

SEAN MAC DERMOTT

THE BULLY'S ACRE KILMAINHAM WAS FOR CENTURIES THE BURIAL GROUND FOR DUBLINERS AND IN THE LAST CENTURY IT WAS FREQUENTED BY BODY SNATCHERS.

THE ROYAL HOSPITAL KILMAINHAM, THE NATIONAL CENTRE FOR CULTURE AND ARTS IN IRELAND, WAS BUILT IN 1680 TO THE DESIGNS OF WLM. ROBINSON. IT STANDS ON THE SITE OF THE CELTIC CHURCH OF MHAIGHNEANN AND LATER THE PRIORY OF THE KNIGHTS HOSPITALLERS.

J WREN

Killester

The Townland of Killester takes its name from Cill Lasera, or Church of St. Lasera. There is a tradition that St. Brigid of Kildare, while on a visit to the convent of Lasera here performed several miracles. When St. Patrick and his followers appeared at the convent their supply problem was solved by just one such of her miracles.

From the 5th to the 9th centuries all north County Dublin was in the Kingdom of Meath and the church at Killester was an appendage of the monastery at Swords. During this period the dedication was transferred from St. Lasera to St. Brigid. Before the Norman invasion the appendage appears to have been transferred again, to the possession of Christ Church cathedral as Quillastra.

In 1174 the prior of the cathedral granted the lands to Audeon Le Brun, an Anglo-Norman adventurer and follower of Henry II. A condition of the grant was the annual payment of 40 pence and a pair of slippers on the altar of Christ Church. A confirmation of the grant by St. Laurence O'Toole to William de Brun in 1178 added the stipulation of a payment of half an ounce of gold and a pair of boots to the Prior annually in Christ Church, as well as the tithes of the land. De Brun did not live long to enjoy his estates, being murdered in 1199.

In the 14th century the White family were in occupation of Killester and a century later the Howth family came into possession when Alice, a daughter of Nicholas White, married Nicholas Saint Lawrence. In 1492, during the bitter feud between the Houses of Ormonde and Kildare, Nicholas, Lord of Howth, entertained Sir James Butler, a scion of the Ormonde faction, at his mother's house at Killester. During the dinner Butler made disparaging remarks of the Earl of Kildare which resulted in Lord Howth throwing down the gauntlet. He is reputed to have told Lord Butler, "I swear by Our Lady of the north church of Howth, that butler, nor winedrawer, nor tapster is not in Ireland, but I daren't stand to defend this quarrel. And if your Lordship be so stomached and would ease your heart, let us both take a boat and go to yonder island of Clontarf, there to ease your stomach and mine, for our companies here are not indifferent". Sir James Butler did not accept the challenge, but departed in a fury saying that Lord Howth's

"stout and bullish nature" would end his days before the natural time.

In the mid 16th century, Thomas Plunkett was resident at Killester. In the same century Thomas Allen, who had benefitted from the confiscated lands of the Knights of the Order of St. John at Clontarf, also lived at Killester. In 1654 Lord Howth was in possession of 140 arable acres, 40 acres of pasture and 6 acres of meadow at Killester. On the premises there was "one faire stone house, slated, with several houses and offices and a stone bawne". At the time of the 1659 census Colonel Chidley Coote, the second son of the fanatical Cromwellian general, Sir Charles Coote, was the principal resident at Killester. The Coote family remained in the area for 40 years and probably built Killester House. In 1697 Lord Howth demised the house, town and lands of Killester to John Bell. The last of the Cootes to reside there had been the late Sir Phipps Coote.

In 1740 a Dubln banker named Thomas Gleadowe was in possession of a landholding at Killester which, on his death, passed to his banker son, William. In 1722 William Gleadowe married Charlotte Newcomen, the only daughter of Charles Newcomen of Carriglass, Co. Longford. In consequence to this alliance, Gleadowe assumed the arms and name of the Newcomens and, in 1778, added Sycamore Park and the Horse Park to his properties at Killester. In 1781 he was knighted and held a seat in the Irish Parliament for Co. Longford. In 1800 Sir William Gleadowe Newcomen sold his vote for the Act of Union and in recognition of her husband's services Dame Charlotte Gleadowe Newcomen was made a peeress.

Sir William died in 1807 to be succeeded by his son, Thomas Viscount Newcomen, who was educated at Eton and Oxford and was admitted to the Bar at Lincoln Inns in 1794. He became a chief

partner in the family bank at Castle Street and was described by W. J. Fitzpatrick, the author of "The Secret Service under Pitt", as a pervert and reprobate. Stories circulated about how the miserly Newcomen spent many nights in Castle Street Bank (now the Dublin corporation's rates offices) gloating over the riches deposited within. In 1825 however, Newcomen's bank collapsed and many customers were financially ruined and, in the same year, Thomas Viscount Newcomen committed suicide at Killester House.

Nothing remains today of the mediaeval church of St. Brigid in the ancient churchyard on Killester Avenue, except a rough outline of its foundations. When Gabriel Beranger sketched the church in 1769 the building had already been in a state of ruin for over a century. Beranger's drawing (now in the National Library) shows a quadrangular roofless building with gothic window openings and thick walls, which measured 46 feet long and 17 feet wide.

A number of memorial stones in the old churchyard indicate the preference of 18th century city merchants and tradesmen for interment in rural burial grounds. During the days of the "sack 'em ups" the secluded cemetery was, like its neighbour in Artane, the scene of regular nocturnal visitations by grave robbers.

The modern church of St. Brigid's, on the Howth Road, was blessed and dedicated on September 27th, 1926. This church contains a relic of Saint Brigid. A portion of her head was returned to Ireland from Portugal in 1927. A fine painting of the profession of St. Mel by St. Brigid, the work of the late George Collie RHA, was completed here in 1952.

An old convent is marked on the 1837 ordnance survey map on a site to the rear of the present church. It is thought that the convent may have been founded

(Continued on Page 98)

KILLESTER

WHEN NICHOLAS, LORD OF HOWTH, ENTERTAINED SIR JAMES BUTLER AT HIS MOTHER'S HOUSE AT KILLESTER IN 1492 HE CHALLENGED HIM TO A DUEL WHEN BUTLER ATTACKED THE EARL OF KILDARE'S CONDUCT.

SIR THOMAS NEWCOMEN

FURRY PARK HOUSE

KILLESTER HOUSE

HOME OF BANKER SIR WILLIAM GLEADOWE NEWCOMEN AND HIS SON SIR THOMAS NEWCOMEN. WHEN THE FAMILY BANK FELL IN 1825 SIR THOMAS NEWCOMEN DIED BY HIS OWN HAND HERE. KILLESTER HOUSE WAS DESTROYED BY FIRE IN 1919.

ONE OF THE FEW 18TH CENT. MEDIUM SIZED COUNTRY HOUSES IN THE DUBLIN AREA WAS BUILT BY BANKER JOSEPH FADE IN 1730. THE HOUSE WAS THE SUBJECT OF A RECENT RESTORATION ORDER.

J.WREN

Lucan

Leamhcan

(Place of the Elms)

Lucan was once famous for its sulphur spa. In the eighteenth century all the leading figures of Dublin society would visit the picturesque village built at the confluence of the Liffey with its little tributary, the river Griffin, to take the waters. Today the name of the Spa Hotel is the only reminder of its earlier fame.

Lucan's history stretches back to the earliest chronicles of Irish history. The Esker ridge outside the town is part of the boundary agreed between Conn of the Hundred Battles and Eoghan Mor which split Ireland along a line running roughly between present day Dublin and Galway. Conn ruled north of the line and Eoghan Mor south of it.

The village of Lucan was also important from early times as a crossing point of the Liffey and for its salmon weirs. In the early Christian era there was a church here and the Normans built a castle to dominate the crossing in the 12th century. The ancient ruins of the church at Esker, overlooking the village, date from this period. In mediaeval times Esker was one of the four royal manors of County Dublin and in the last century there was a grammar school and cotton factory there.

The churchyard at Esker was the burial place of Fr James McCaratan, a local Catholic curate who was murdered on the Hill of Lucan in June 1807. He was the victim of a gang of robbers who waylaid and shot him as he returned home from a visit to Palmerstown. Two members of the gang, Christopher Walsh aged 34 and Thomas Weir, aged 19, were shortly afterwards apprehended and found guilty of perpetrating the crime. They were hanged on the spot where the crime was committed, the custom of the time, but three other gang members avoided capture.

During the 12th century the lands of Lucan were given to an Alard FitzWilliam but he granted them in turn to a Wirris Peche, who was confirmed in his possession by King John in 1204 on payment of 40 marks and the presentation of a palfrey to the king's treasurer.

Peche, whose family was of Saxon origin, came from Hampshire and his family retained possession of Lucan until the fourteenth century. In 1305 Roesia Peche, probably his great granddaughter, and her husband, John Hanstede, were involved in a law suit over salmon fisheries on the Liffey with their cousins the Pippards, owners of Leixlip. They lost the lawsuit, in which the King also was a plaintiff. Half their salmon fishery had to be surrendered to the Pippards and a weir erected by a Roger Smalris was removed because it narrowed the waterway and was prejudicial to the King's rights on the river.

By 1327 Robert de Nottingham, a former Mayor of Dublin and one of its wealthiest citizens, had acquired the Lucan estate and on his death, shortly afterwards, he left a well furnished house with much livestock, including 1,000 sheep and 200 lambs.

In the sixteenth century it was the property of the earls of Kildare. In 1517 Elizabeth, wife of Garret, ninth earl of Kildare, died in Lucan castle. It was confiscated when his son rebelled against the crown and leased, in 1554, to the Clerk of the Check of the Army, Matthew King, on condition that he occupied the castle himself and manned it with soldiers at his own expense. The latter were to use only the English language and dress as a condition of the grant.

Shortly afterwards the castle and estate fell into the ownership of their most famous landlords, the Sarsfields. Originally from Herefordshire, the family arrived in Ireland after the Anglo-Norman invasion and lived for a time at Sarsfieldstown in County Meath. Successful businessmen, several members of the family were mayors of Dublin. The most famous of the latter was William Sarsfield, who was knighted in 1566 for driving off Ulster rebels threatening Drogheda during the absence of the Lord Deputy, Sir Henry Sidney. Shortly afterwards Sarsfield was deprived of his citizenship of Dublin for abandoning his town house in favour of Lucan, during a visitation of the plague on the city.

Nevertheless, in 1571, he was called upon to serve as County Sheriff and led several military expeditions outside the Pale, mainly to pursue rebels in County Wicklow. An outspoken critic of the crown himself, he was also imprisoned in Dublin Castle for a time with other local dignatories for protesting at the high taxes imposed to pursue Queen Elizabeth I's wars in Ireland. He outlived his immediate heirs and died in 1616 aged 96.

Like other Dublin villages Lucan witnessed many of the most dramatic events of the wars of the confederacy of Kilkenny in the 1640s. In 1646 General Preston occupied the village and had protracted negotiations with the Earl of Clanricarde on behalf of King Charles II and also with the Papal Nuncio, Rinunccini for the rebels. Preston eventually made agreements with both, later reneging on that to Clanricarde.

In 1689, during James II's 'Patriot Parliament', one of the junior members was Patrick Sarsfield, who was shortly to become the deposed monarch's ablest military commander in the Williamite wars. James was later to make him Earl of Lucan for his services but he was not recognised as such by the victorious Williamites. His most famous exploit was the night ride from Limerick during the city's siege to destroy the Williamite siege train and artillery at Ballyneety.

Like many other defeated Jacobites he followed his deposed monarch, James II into French exile. He rose to become a marshall of France under Louis XIV and died in 1693 at the battle of Landen, reputedly with the words on his lips, "Would to God this had been for Ireland".

His son married a daughter of the Earl of Clanricarde but died without issue in 1719. The estates passed through Sarsfield's niece Charlottee (who was also a grand daughter of Louis XIV), to the Vesey family when she married Agmondisham Vesey. Their grandson, the Rt Hon Agmondesham Vesey of Lucan was a good friend of Samuel Johnson and Edmund Burke. It was this Vesey who built Lucan House, now the home of the Italian ambassador, alongside the old castle whose ruins remain in the grounds. In the words of Francis Elrington Ball, the doyen of Dublin's local historians, 'Lucan House stands as a monument to Vesey's skill in design, its Ionic front and hall adorned with pillars and a freize in the Grecian order and enriched with medallions from designs by Angelica Kauffman, having received encomiums from good judges". The latter included the great architect, Sir William Chambers. It was completed in 1772.

Vesey's building projects attracted less favourable mention from Dean

(Continued on Page 98)

LUCAN

LUCAN HOUSE

LUCAN CASTLE

PATRICK SARSFIELD THE GREAT IRISH GENERAL WHO WAS BORN AT LUCAN CASTLE IN 1650 LED THE ATTACK ON THE WILLIAMITE GUN TRAIN AT BALLYNEETY. HE DIED FROM HIS WOUNDS AT THE BATTLE OF LANDEN IN 1693.

THE FAMOUS LUCAN SPA WAS A POPULAR RENDEZVOUS FOR DUBLIN SOCIETY IN THE 18TH CENTURY WHERE A BALLROOM WAS ERECTED.

THE ARCHITECT, JAMES GANDON DIED AT HIS HOME CANNONBROOK, LUCAN IN 1823.

AT ESKER IS THE COMMENCEMENT OF A LINE OF LOW HILLS WHICH STRETCHES TO CO. GALWAY. IN THE 2ND CENTURY CONN OF THE HUNDRED BATTLES AND OWEN MOR AGREED TO THE ESKER RIADA AS THE DEVIDING LINE OF IRELAND.

J. WREN

Malahide

Mullach Ide

The Hill of the Hydes

Malahide, like Dalkey, ranks amongst the earliest sites of human settlement in Ireland. Thousands of flint tools and arrowheads have been found at Paddy's Hill near the village. Its earliest inhabitants were mesolithic hunters who arrived around 7500 BC and neolithic farmers had occupied the area by 3500 BC. By then pottery was being made and the farmers built a fortified refuge on Feltrim Hill nearby.

Not surprisingly Malahide features in the Leabhar Gabhala, or Book of Invasions as the landfall of the Fir Domhnainn. The place where they landed, Inbhir Domainn, has survived in the local place-names of Moll Downeys Bank and Downey Creek. Seamount is an anglicisation of Suidhe Manannaan and the seagod, Manannan Mac Lir was the legendary ruler of the area and was defeated in combat by Finn at the short deeps.

Nuada of the Silver Arm, King of the Tuatha De Danann, is also closely associated with the area and the No-den mound off Seamount Road bears his name. Paddy's Hill is named after St Patrick, who is reputed to have preached there.

Because of its position on the Broadwater estuary it was almost inevitable that Malahide would share the fate of Baldoyle and other coastal Dublin villages in becomingg a base for the viking raiders of the 8th, 9th and 10th centuries. In 897 they destroyed the great monastery of Glassmore outside Swords. But unlike many neigbouring places, such as Lambay, Howth, Baldoyle and Balgriffin, Malahide did not lose its old Irish name.

The Norse control of Malahide, like much of Fingal, remained unshaken until the arrival of the Anglo-Norman invaders. The village was captured by the invaders in an 'amphibious' operation involving a simultaneous attacking on the Viking garrison by land and by sea. A Norman knight, Sir Richard Talbot, was subsequently granted the right of judgement, of water and iron, the duel, the pit and the gallows, and Lord High Admiral of the seas of Malahide' for ever in return for the supply to the king of one archer with a horse and coat of mail whenever required.

He built a traditional Norman motte and bailey which was quickly replaced by a stone castle around 1200. The family continued to live there until 1976 when the last Baron Talbot de Malahide died without issue. His sister, the Honourable Rose Talbot de Malahide emigrated to Australia after disposing of the castle to the state and its contents were auctioned off. Today the castle and its grounds are a major amenity for the people of Fingal and it is maintained by Dublin County Council. The late Lord Talbot

was an important diplomat in the British service and in the course of many foreign postings he collected rare plants. Today the gardens contain no less than 4,500 different species.

The castle is also associated with what has been described as the most important of all literary discoveries – the Boswell papers. A great grand daughter of James Boswell, the friend and biographer of Dr Johnson, married the fifth Baron of Malahide in the nineteenth century and subsequently, when the main line of the Boswell family died out in 1917 various items were bequeathed to the Malahide branch. Professor Chauncy B Tinker of Yale University received an anonymous tip-off in the early 1920s that there were many valuable documents at Malahide Castle. Over the next three decades three of Boswell's journals, over 1,300 of his letters, one of his manuscripts and over 100 of Johnson's letters were retrieved. Much of the material was found stuffed into old furniture. The whole lot was subsequently sold privately to Yale University, where it is catalogued and stored today. Amongst the furniture was a fine 17th century Flemish ebony cabinet, known today as the Boswell cabinet, it is on public display at the castle.

In recent years another important discovery has been the papers of the merchant Nathaniel Trumbell, which were stored in old trunks at Beechwood House in Malahide. Covering every aspect of 18th and 19th century life, this collection is considered one of the finest historical finds in Ireland.

The ruins of a mediaeval church stand in the grounds of the castle and built into it are Sheela-na-Gig figures. These fantastic carved figures of naked women date back to Celtic times and were meant to scare away the devil. Many Norman church builders incorporated them into their own structures to placate ancient spirits and the beliefs of their new parishioners. The Malahide Sheela-na-Gig probably dates to the 8th century. The building also contains a number of tombs including the 15th century altar bomb of Lady Maude Plunkett, the wife of Sir Richard Talbot de Malahide. She had earlier been married to Sir Walter Hussey, son of the Baron of Galtrim – for one day. During the wedding feast word was brought that a raiding party was in

the vicinity and Sir Walter joined the defenders of the village only to be killed in the ensuing battle. His wife was therefore a "maid, wife and widow", in one day. She was subsequently the heroine of a popular poem 'The Bridal of Malahide' by Gerald Griffin.

The holy well at the rear of St Sylvester's Church in Malahide also dates back to early times. The name Sylvester may apply to the Roman bishop of the 4th century or to Silvanus, the pagan sun god. It may also have been named after Pope Sylvester, the 10th century French pope, by the conquering Normans. The well was reputed to have medicinal properties and up until the end of the last century a tradition of placing an eel in the well each year to purify its waters was an annual event. Recently the well was restored by the Old Malahide Society.

The modern St Sylvester's church was built in 1837 in the neogothic style. When it was dedicated on Sunday July 5th, 1846, His Grace Archbishop Murray of Dublin presided and the great apostle of temperance, the Rev Theobald Matthew, delivered a sermon and administered the pledge to many present. In 1903 a magnificent new high altar was consecrated in St Sylvester's, which was the work of William J Pearse of the firm of Pearse and Sons. He executed the whole structure with the exception of the tabernacle panels and agony in the garden group which were from the chisel of his father James Pearse, whose sons Patrick and Willie (above) were to be executed in 1916. The two carved heads supporting the arch over the front door of St Sylvester's are said to represent saint Brigid and Colmcille. The spire, designed by George Ashlin, is a late addition dating to 1901 and is said to be modelled on that of All Saints church in Raheny.

Because of its location Malahide was a pioneering centre for tide mills in the era before chemical fuels were available in abundance. Dr William Petty, physician to Cromwell's army in Ireland reported in the 1650s that Malahide had "a mill that goeth by ebb tides". Ireland had ten tide mills of which four were at Malahide and two of the rest at Portmarnock. The great drawback of tide mills is that they must be worked when the tide is running out and this makes for irregular

(Continued on Page 99)

MALAHIDE

THE EARLIEST RECORDED PEOPLE TO SETTLE IN MALAHIDE WERE A SEPT OF GAULISH CELTS CALLED THE FIR DOMHNAINN

MALAHIDE CASTLE

"THE JOY BELLS ARE RINGING IN GAY MALAHIDE"

LADY MAUDE PLUNKETT BIDS FAREWELL TO HER HUSBAND

ROBS WALLS MALAHIDE

MANORIAL CHURCH OF ST. SYLVESTER

J. WREN

Marino

Before the building of the Marino housing estate in the 1920s some acres of open ground here were known as the Bloody Fields. Some of the fiercest hand-to-hand fighting during the battle of Clontarf took place here. Reference to it is made by the Rev Dillon Cosgrave in his 'North Dublin and its Environs'. He states that some of the vestiges of Tomar's wood still survived at Marino and Clontarf Castle.

The name Marino only dates from the mid-18th century. Before Lord Charlemont developed his magnificent estate the lands formed part of the Donnycarney townland. In former times a village stood between Drumcondra and present day Marino called Goose Green, which was named after the Goose Green in south-east London. In his Dublin guide of 1787 Richard Lewis, an English writer, described it as "a small village a mile beyond Drumcondra and two-and-a-half miles from Dublin Castle".

The only remnants of the village are two houses standing in Grace Park Terrace near Griffith Avenue called Upton Lodge and Ivy Lodge. A native of Goose Green was Christopher Clinton Hoey, who was born in 1829 and became wellknown journalist in London, where he died in 1885. He contributed to the 'Irish Builder' and wrote a series for it on 'Unknown Dublin' in 1872.

Upton Lodge was built in the late 18th century by Mayor Upton and was only accessible by Goose Green Road, now Grace Park Road. Amongst its subsequent residents were several leading 19th century lawyers such as George W White, James Magee and Thomas Perrin Davies. In Easter Week one of its residents, Terry Simpson left the Lodge to take his place as a Volunteer in the College of Surgeons garrison and his sister Tillie served in the GPO.

Ivy Lodge was built slightly later, in the 1830s, by Peter Walsh. Another house built nearby was Sally Park, which gave its name to the area around the top of Philipsburgh Avenue for a time. Its first occupants were the Butterly family. In the late 1800s Goose Green was a favourite venue for Irish-style wrestling bouts.

In 1906 the Catholic University GAA club acquired Croydon Park's grounds for playing fields and for some years it was the venue of games, fetes, carnivals and band recitals. In 1914 the house and lands were leased to the Irish Transport and General Workers' Union as a recreational centre

Sean O'Casey, in his 'Story of the Irish Citizen Army' tells how hard drilling was followed by dancing, piping and singing which kept the night perpetually young. A rifle range was set up and members of the newly formed Irish Citizen Army

practised here after the Howth gun running operation. Jim Larkin lived in Croydon Park House and Constance Markiewicz and James Connolly were amongst the frequent visitors.

The most significant landmark of the area remains the Casino, which was built by Lord Charlmont. It was in 1755 when James Caulfield, Earl of Charlemont, returned from his European tour and took over a modest house and the small estate of Marino as his home. It had been a present of his stepfather, Thomas Adderly, a Bandon based politician and industrialist who built the house two years earlier. Mrs Delaney, the diarist, reported seeing it being constructed in 1753. Called Marino House, it survived until the 1920s. Of elegant appearance it measured only 60 feet square but had a fine gallery. Several later additions were made under the supervision of Sir William Chambers, who also designed the Casino.

James Caulfield, the fourth viscount and first Earl of Charlemont, was descended from an Oxfordshire family. His ancestor, Captain Toby Caulfield came to Ireland as an Elizabethan adventurer in the service of the Earl of Essex in 1599. He commanded Charlemont Fort in Armagh and was knighted for his services in 1603, becoming Baron Charlemont in 1623. The family prospered in Ireland and William Caulfield became a Viscount under Charles II. He extended his protection to Saint Oliver Plunkett during the vice royalty of Lord Berkeley.

James Caulfield, the first Earl of Charlemont, was born in the family home at Jervis Street on August 18th, 1728. The hospital now stands on the site. Six years later he inherited the title of fourth Viscount on his father's death. He was a sickly child and was educated by a tutor, the Rev Edward Murphy, "a gentleman of considerable classical attainments". In 1746, accompanied by the Rev Murphy, he set out on a nine year long European tour. During this period he studied at Messina and kept a journal of his travels which are of important historical value because of his scholarly accomplishments. Recently an account of his time in Greece and Turkey was published and makes interesting reading.

On his return to settle at Marino he extended the property by acquiring several adjoining farms. With the aid of

Matthew Peters, a consultant gardener, he set out to beautify his estate overlooking Dublin Bay with parklands and gardens. The Casino was the crowning glory of the gardens. It was designed by Chambers and Simon Vierpyl was brought from Rome to Dublin in 1756 to build it. The Casino was completed around 1772.

This palladian building is a Greek cross in plan and contains eight rooms in the basement, four state rooms on the ground floor and four bedrooms on the first floor. In the miniscule study there is a tint dome around which are the signs of the zodiac. The doors and richly carved door cases have recently been restored to their full splendour. The casino has two wings with porticos to each side with attic storeys on north and south over an entablature. On the north are the statues of Ceres and Bacchus and on the south those of Venus and Apollo which were restored to their original positions after a number of years in the basement. Cipriani also worked on the Casino and executed the lovely ceiling in Lady Charlemont's boudoir and Joseph Wilton did some of the sculptures. Lord Charlemont entertained many distinguished visitors here, including John Wesley. When the founder of Methodism came to Marino in 1778 he remarked on the absence of singing birds near Dublin.

Charlemont's heirs showed little interest in the property. In the mid-19th century a slab of lapis lazuli of great value disappeared from the chimney place and much of the beautiful interior woodwork had been vandalised for firewood. During the War of Independence the semi-derelict building and its numerous underground passages were used by Michael Collins and the Irish Volunteers.

It was not until 1932 that the Casino was placed under State guardianship by the trustees of the adjoining O'Brien Institute and restoration work was begun by Harold Leask, inspector of public monuments. Minor repairs were carried out up to 1950 and over the next two years the dampness problem was eradicated. In 1956 and 1957 work was done to the steps and brickwork and in 1963 interior repairs were completed. Most of this was done under the supervision of

(Continued on Page 68)

MARINO

IN 1014 SOME OF THE FIERCE FIGHTING ON THE FIELD OF CLONTARF TOOK PLACE ABOUT MARINO IN TOMAR'S WOOD.

THE MAGNIFICENT CASINO AT MARINO WAS COMPLETED IN 1771 ON THE ESTATE OF THE EARL OF CHARLEMONT (RIGHT) TO THE DESIGNS OF SIR WILLIAM CHAMBERS

IN THE BEAUTIFUL GROUNDS OF CROYDON PARK, MARINO, THE IRISH CITIZEN ARMY DRILLED AND TRAINED IN THE YEARS BEFORE THE 1916 RISING.

JWREN

Monkstown

Monkstown the adjoining parish to Dun Laoghaire was in pre-reformation days the property of Saint Mary's Abbey, Dublin, (hence the name "Monkstown"). The 6th century Celtic saint, Mochonna is associated with Carrickbrennan, (the original name for this area) and is said to be buried in the old burial ground close to Monkstown Castle.

The Cistercians or white monks as they were commonly called built Monkstown Castle in the 12th or 13th century and it consisted of a mansion house in a large courtyard. High walls enclosed the main buildings and three strong towers were built for defensive purposes.

The Cistercians whose mother house was at Buildwas in Shropshire were skilled agriculturalists and were renowned for their system of tillage. The main portion of the Monkstown lands were cultivated by the monks themselves and the remainder was let to tenants who in return were bound to supply labour to the home farm. The white monks who apart from their expertise as farmers were also skilled fishermen and it was under their auspices that a successful fishery was established at Bullock.

The Monkstown fortress of the white monks was a strong bulwark against the cattle raiding hillsmen who periodically descended from the fastnesses of the Wicklow Mountains on forays. The monks who stationed watchmen in the hills were invariably forewarned of the danger from the mountains and livestock were herded into the safety of the Monkstown Castle barn before the arrival of clansmen.

After the dissolution of the monasteries the castle and lands of Monkstown were granted to Sir John Travers, Master of Ordnance in Ireland. Travers who was Irish born was one of the many military adventurers who amassed large fortunes in this country at the expense of the natives. After Travers Monkstown had several owners including Viscount Baltinglass and Sir Gerald Alymer, both of whom were implicated in the Desmond rebellion. During the troubled years of the mid 17th century the Cheevers family were in occupation at Monkstown and in the winter of 1653 Walter Cheevers and his family were banished to Connaught, his only crime being that he was a Catholic.

The property then went to General Ludlow, the regicide who voted for the death of Charles I, who lived there until the restoration. When Henry Cromwell was made Lord Deputy of Ireland he visited Ludlow at Monkstown where the latter voiced his disapproval of the assumption of the regal state of the Lord Protector. On the restoration of Charles II Ludlow made a hasty departure from Ireland where his property and possessions were confiscated and he died in exile in Switzerland.

In 1660 Walter Cheevers was restored to his estates and at that time the population on the lands at Monkstown was returned as eleven English and fifty-three Irish. The last resident of Monkstown Castle was Councillor O'Neill, M.P. of Clonakilty who occupied it in the latter part of the 18th and early 19th centuries. After the termination of his tenancy Monkstown Castle was allowed to fall into ruin. There is a local tradition that the Irish contingents of the British Army who fought at Fontenoy and Waterloo assembled at Monkstown Castle before embarkation.

Charles Haliday the businessman and historian from Arran Quay bought a house called Fairy Hill in Monkstown in 1834 and nine years later moved into Lord Ranelagh's old mansion, Monkstown Park. Here he built a large Italianite residence where he housed his valuable collection of books, one of the finest in Ireland. When the great Ferdinand de Lesseps came to Ireland in 1855 seeking support for his ideas of linking East and West which culminated in the building of the Suez Canal, he visited Haliday at Monkstown Park.

(Continued from Page 66)

W P de Clerc, assisted latterly by Austin Dunphy. In 1972 the Office of Public Works agreed that the monument should finally be vested in state ownership and in 1974 the firm of architects, O'Neill, Flanagan and Partners were commissioned for its full restoration. Work was completed ten years later and on July 6th, 1984, its doors were opened to the public.

Marino Crescent at the junction of the Malahide Road and Clontarf Road was built around 1792 by Charles Ffolliot, an Aungier Street contractor. The houses were once called "Spite Crescent" by local wags because of a dispute between Ffolliot and Lord Charlemont. Ffolliot was accused of erecting the row of houses to obscure Charlemont's view of Dublin Bay.

When the foundations were dug large quantities of human bones were uncovered, which were thought to be those of

Marino

the fallen at the Battle of Clontarf. This did nothing to discharge The Crescent's popularity as a place of residence. During the 1840s the novelist, William Carleton, lived at No. 2 and he later moved to the less grandiose Marino Cottages on the Malahide Road where he lived at No. 3. He later moved out to Woodville in Sandford where he died in 1869.

Bram Stoker, the author of 'Dracula', first saw the light of day at No. 15 Marino Crescent on November 8th, 1847. He was a sickly child but later developed into a fine athlete and was a champion runner at Trinity. His family moved to Artane Lodge at the then Rural Pucktown Lane when he was four. It is now part of Collins Avenue West. Stoker followed his father Abraham into the civil service but he developed a strong interest in the theatre and became private secretary to the celebrated actor, Henry Irving. He wrote several novels but his terrifying masterpiece of the supernatural, the story of 'Dracula', has placed him amongst the world's greatest horror writers.

Martin Harvey, the author of a 'History of Ireland', a great deal of which was drawn from original documents in the State Paper Office, resided at No. 21 Marino Crescent in the last century. Haverty, who was for many years on the staff of the 'Freeman's Journal', has his name commemorated in the nearby Marino housing estate at Haverty Road.

MONKSTOWN

THE CISTERCIAN MONKS OF SAINT MARY'S ABBEY DUBLIN BUILT MONKS-TOWN CASTLE AND FOR CENTURIES TILLED THE LAND HERE.

CHARLES HALIDAY (BELOW) THE CELEBRATED AUTHOR OF "THE SCANDINAVIAN KINGDOM OF DUBLIN" ENTERTAINED THE GREAT FERDINAND DE LESSEPS OF SUEZ CANAL FAME AT MONKSTOWN PARK IN 1855.

DE LESSEPS

HALIDAY

THERE IS A TRADITION THAT THE IRISH CONTINGENT THAT FOUGHT AT FONTENOY AND WATERLOO ASSEMBLED AT MONKSTOWN CASTLE.

JWREN

Portmarnock

Port Mearnog

Like neighbouring Malahide, Portmarnock is one of the oldest inhabited settlements in Ireland. Flint implements found in fields near the village date back to at least 3000 BC. It is reputed to be part of the Magh an Ealta of Keating's Forus Feasa ar Éirinn, where Nin son of Bel landed 4,000 years ago in the one spot of Ireland not covered by trees. Forests were a far greater obstacle to settlement by primitive peoples than we can easily imagine today.

It is referred to again during the death of Partholon as Sean Mhagh Ealta Eadar, or the old plain of the flocks of Eadair. Seabirds still gather on the estuary between Portmarnock and Howth. Successive waves of invaders first arrived along this stretch of coast (see Malahide) and the last of these in prehistoric times were the Magh Bhregha or Bregia, a Celtic tribe related to the Brigantes of northern Britain. They arrived around 350 BC and settled on the whole east coast between the Liffey and the Mournes. Portmarnock later became part of the kingdom of Meath.

In Saint Patrick's time the dominant sept in Portmarnock were the Cianachta and the first church in the area was erected by a local saint Marnock who was a member of the family. The present ruined church on the site, which lies between the Strand Road and the sea, was built by the Anglo-Norman invaders. Between it and the road lies St Marnock's well. At one time it had 16 stone steps down to it and an Ogham pillar. To the north side was a willow whose branches were bent over the well during the storms, when local people believed the leaves whispered prayers for the safety of fishermen. In the last century the well was filled in and a pump built. The pump's foundation and a concrete water trough are all that remain today.

At the end of the 8th century the Vikings came. In 795 they plundered offshore Lambay Island and shortly afterwards they occupied Portmarnock and the adjoining coastal villages. Hamund Mac Turkill, the last Norse king of Dublin owned Portmarnock as part of his personal estate and after his defeat and death by the Anglo-Norman invaders in 1171 his lands here were given to St Mary's Abbey. The area suffered again in 1349 when Portmarnock and all the east coast of Fingal was devastated by the Black Death. The estates remained in the possession of St Mary's Abbey until the dissolution of the monasteries by Henry VIII in the 1530s. Patrick Barnewall of Fieldstown remained loyal to Henry VIII and received a grant of some of the best land in north county Dublin, including Turvey and the "mill near Portmarnock commonly called the Grange of Portnarmock."

During the wars of Elizabeth I later in the century this area was frequently despoiled and in 1630 Archbishop Lancelot Bulkleley described the old Norman church as being in a ruinous condition. He also complained that the area was full of recusants and that mass was said regularly at the home of Sir Walter Plunkett at the Grange.

In the survey of Ireland ordered by Oliver Cromwell in 1654 Portmarnock was described as consisting of four farms, one of 358 acres owned by William Plunkett, one of 360 acres owned by Walter Plunkett and two consisting of 240 acres owned by Nicholas Barnewall. Each contained at least one slated house, usually in poor condition and a small village of between six and ten thatched cottages. On Barnewall's larger farm was a tide mill and on the second, at Robswalls, was "One Castle wth a thacht house adjoyning a Barne & Stable thacht". The Census of 1659 listed a total of 32 persons living at Portmarnock, seven English and 25 Irish and Roger Bishop Esq and George Usher, Gentleman.

Both the Barnewalls and the Plunketts, like many of the old English gentry remained papists and lost their lands in the wars of the 17th century. The last of the Barnewalls, Matthew, left Ireland after the Treaty of Limerick and died fighting for Louis XIV at the battle of Rouamont in 1692, while serving in the Duke of Berwick's regiment.

The village grew in the more peaceful 18th and early 19th century to reach a total of 631 by the time of the first Census in 1841, but it declined during the rest of the 1800s to little more than 400 souls, probably due to emigration and the decline of the local fishing industry. In Griffith's land valuation of 1848 about a quarter of the parochial land area was wasteland around The Borrough but the remainder was described as good quality and worth between £4 and £6 an acre.

In more recent times the most famous

aspects of Portmarnock have been its two mile beach, the Velvet Strand and the adjoining golf course. The strand became a mecca for world class aviators in the early 1930s, attracted by its firm and perfectly level surface which made it the longest natural runway in Europe. In 1930 the Australian air ace, Sir Charles Kingsford-Smith, made a successful east-west crossing of the Atlantic from the Velvet Strand in 'The Southern Cross' in a round the world' trip. His navigator was Captain Patrick Saul of the Irish air corps, a Skerries man. Jim Mollison, the 'Flying Scot' and husband of Amy Johnson – the first woman to fly around the world – flew the first solo east-west crossing of the Atlantic from Portmarnock in August 1932. His plane was 'The Heart's Content'. The following year another Australian pilot, Charles Ulm, brought 'Faith in Australia' to Portmarnock for a similar attempt. Unfortunately one of the wheels sank into a soft patch of sand and, as gardai and local people tried to lift it, a wing broke off injuring several onlookers and the attempt had to be abandoned.

The nearby golf courses was opened on St Stephen's Day 1894 and the first Open Championship took place in 1899. A professional tournament was organised in 1910 with a prize fund of £225. The first Irish Open was held in 1927 and won by George Duncan. Since then Portmarnock has become one of the world's premier courses.

The Velvet Strand was also famous as a training ground for racehorses, although the village is better known today for the harness racing track off the main Dublin-Malahide Road and the strand itself has become a major resort for Dubliners in the summer.

In the early 20th century members of the Gaelic League were amongst the first daytrippers to make picnic outings to the resort. In 1906 the inaugural event of the Motorcycling Union of Ireland (Dublin Centre) took place at Portmarnock Strand, when the one mile handicap was won by C.W. Lewis with A.J. Kettle second.

One of the finest buildings in Portmarnock is the Country Club. This is the former home of the Jameson family of whiskey fame. John Jameson was a

(Continued on Page 100)

PORTMARNOCK

SAINT MARNOCK WHO WAS FOUNDER OF A CHURCH AT PORTMARNOCK WAS ALSO FAMOUS THROUGHOUT SCOTLAND WHERE HIS NAME IS PRESERVED IN KILMARNOCK AND INCHMARNOCK

THE ANCIENT CHURCH RUIN AT PORTMARNOCK DATES FROM THE 12TH OR 13TH CENTURY AND WAS IN USE UNTIL 1615

THE SHERIFF OF DUBLIN TOOK POSSESSION OF 8 BUTTS OF WINE WHICH HAD BEEN CAST ASHORE AT PORTMARNOCK FROM A SHIPWRECK IN 1465. THE ABBOT HANDCOCK OF SAINT MARY'S ABBEY HOWEVER BECAUSE OF THIS ENCROACHMENT ON ABBEY LAND COMPELLED THE SHERIFFS OFFICERS TO SURRENDER THE WINE.

AT THE WORLD FAMOUS CHAMPIONSHIP GOLF COURSE OF PORTMARNOCK GEORGE DUNCAN WON THE FIRST IRISH OPEN IN 1927.

J. WREN

Rath Eanna

Eanna's Fort)

John D'Alton visiting Raheny in the 1830s described it as "picturesquely situated amidst old trees on the brow of an eminence crowned by a little church". The church was St. Assam's, the ruins of which now lie in the village centre. The ruins also mark the site of the rath, or fort of Eanna, from which the parish takes its name.

History is silent about the deeds of Eanna but he was most likely a local Celtic headman or chieftain.

St. Assam's church was built in the year 1712 on the site of an earlier church of which we know nothing. It is believed that St. Assam (or Assan), the patron of Raheny, was a disciple of St. Patrick. A skilled metalworker he became the first bishop of Elphin in Roscommn.

Other distinguised clerics of the parish include Henry Grattan's grandfather, the Rev. Patrick Grattan, who was rector of Raheny for many years and the Rev. Richard Graves, a fellow of Trinity College who consecutively held the chairs or oratory, Greek and divinity. He was rector of Raheny in 1809.

From the Creidi Midhi we learn that the church in Raheny had belonged to the Priory of the Church of the Holy Trinity (Christchurch) in earlier times, and later to St. Mary's Abbey. At the dissolution of the monasteries in the 16th century the St. Lawrence family of Howth acquired the Raheny lands.

In November 1781 the old churchyard was the scene of a strange midnight burial, for it transpired that the coffin lowered into the grave was full of bricks. The man who was supposed to have been buried was one John Lonergan, who was sentenced to death for assisting in the murder of his employer, Captain O'Flaherty of Clare Street.

Apparently by bribing his executioner Lonergan received a mock hanging at Baggot St. gallows. With the aid of friends he made good his escape to America.

The church of All Saints, Howth Road, Raheny, which replaced the older St. Assam's as the Church of Ireland parish church in 1889, is a very elaborate gothic eficice on the lines of a mini-Salisbury Cathedral. Edmond Arthur Guinness, Lord Ardilaun (who is buried in its vault) financed the building.

It was carried out by the Collen Brothers of Portadown, to the design of the great Victorian architect George Ashlin. "The Irish Builder" of 1888 had the following to say of it: "Fingal has no church to compare with its perfectness of detail and generaly symmetry of its proportions, and in these particulars it is one of the most interesting churches in Ireland".

The church is cruciform in structure, measuring 75 feet from East to West and 47 feet at its greatest breadth. The outer walls are built of granite with limestone dressings.

The floor is in Irish oak blocks and ceramic mosaic, while the roof is of pitch pine. The tower is in three stages and is surmounted by an octagonal spire with angle turrets and is 110 feet in height.

The pulpit of well seasoned oak is a fine specimen of wood carving which was executed by A.P. Sharpe of Great Brunswick Street, the partner of James Pearse (father of the 1916 leader). The entire cost of the work was £9,000.

In less peaceful times Raheny gained notoriety as the fief of Sir John De Courcy. In the year 1182 he set out from here to conquer Ulster with a handful of mail clad warriors. He was accompanied by his brother-in-law Sir Tristram St. Lawrence.

During the 1641 rebellion it was reported that "divers of the inhabitants of Raheny, Kilbarrack and Clontarf had declared themselves rebels, having robbed and spoiled some of His Majesty's good subjects (they) are now assembled thereabouts in great numbers mustering and training". A party of soldiers under the command of the bloodthirsty Sir Charles Coote was subsequently despatched by the Duke of Ormond to cut off the rebels and raid and despoil their homes.

In more normal times the villages witnessed the annual ceremony of Riding to the Franchises. From the middle ages onwards several hundred horsemen in fine array accompanied the Lord Mayor, Sheriff and members of the corporation who would ride to mark the city boundary on August 1st every year.

The small brook which is now skirted by Watermill Lane was then the most northern limit of the city's jurisdiction. The occasion was always accompanied by a colourful pageant.

In 1592 Christopher St. Lawrence, the Earl of Howth who was known as the Blind Lord, built a house at Raheny which bore the family coat of arms and those of his wife, Elizabeth Plunkett.

When visiting Watermill Lane in 1837 John D'Alton found this stone built into an angle of a Mr. Papworth's cottage. It is now in Howth castle.

George Papworth, whose house stood near the seafront, was a distinguished architect. He designed many fine buildings in the city including the Carmelite church in Whitefriar's Street, the Abbey Presbyterian Church, the King's Bridge and the tomb of John Philpott Curran, who defended many of the '98 rebels.

Another old house which once stood in this area was Watermill House, where William Boland, founder of Boland's bakery, lived.

Bettyglen House, one of the finest residences in Dublin, was built overlooking the sea at Watermill Road by the Jameson Whiskey family in 1910. It is still standing.

Other notable buildings in Raheny included the Manor House on the site where the convent school of the order of the Poor Servants of the Mother of God stands.

Richard Kelly JP, close friend of Daniel O'Connell and champion of Catholic emancipation, lived at the Manor House from 1844 for many years.

The Church of Ireland school and master's house formerly stood in the main street and the teacher here was Robert Armstrong, well known in the last century for his many interesting topographical articles in the Dublin Penny Journal.

(Continued on Page 84)

RAHENY
ENNA'S FORT

RAHENY TAKES ITS NAME FROM THE FORT OF EANNA WHO WAS PROBABLY THE CHIEFTAIN OF THE DISTRICT IN ANCIENT TIMES.

ALL SAINTS CHURCH (C. OF I.) RAHENY

IN THE SUMMER OF 1182 JOHN DE COURCY THE NORMAN LORD OF RAHENY SET FORTH FROM HERE TO CONQUER ULSTER.

J. WREN '91

DESIGNED IN THE VICTORIAN GOTHIC STYLE BY GEORGE ASHLIN.

Ranelagh

Ranelagh was one of the many manors that comprised the see of Dublin in the middle ages and much of it was covered by Cullenswood. The district's earliest name was Colon and its earliest residents were the archbishops of Dublin and their servants at Nova Colonia.

The presence of the prelates did nothing to inhibit the activities of the Wicklow septs, who frequently used the cover of the wood for raids on Dublin. Here, on Easter Monday 1209, a group of English settlers from Bristol were massacred by the O'Tooles. The Bristolians had retired to the wood for sports and entertainment. In 1316 David O'Toole spent a night in the wood planning a similar raid, but the citizens of Dublin were alerted and sallied out under Sir William Comyn to defeat the Wicklowmen, killing many of them.

The archbishops of Dublin issued many decrees from Nova Colonia. In 1290 Archbishop John de Sanford, who was also Justiciary of Ireland, received a deputation of Dublin merchants there. The area suffererd badly during the invasion of Ireland by the Bruces and, in 1316, the Archbishop's hall, chamber and chapel were described as having been gutted with fire and levelled to the ground, along with the kitchens, farmhouses, stable and granary. The pastures were destroyed and even Cullenswood was severely ravaged. The archbishop's serfs had run off and, finding it impossible to recover them, he leased the lands to an English farmer, Richard Chamberlain.

In the 16th century the lands came into the possession of the FitzWilliams, Tudor viceroys and adventurers in Ireland. The first was Thomas Fitz-William, who also held the office of keeper of Cullenswood. Sir William Ussher of Donnybrook owned the wood in the early 17th century and at the time of the great rebellion in 1641 it was the property of Thomas Ward, a yeoman. In 1642 his house and lands were burnt by rebels, who also drove off a bull, 16 cows and eight horses. A neighbour, Thomas Parnell who was a goldsmith, was taken prisoner by the rebel leader, another O'Toole, and held for ransome in Arklow.

In the 18th century Willbrook became the main local residence and the Right Reverend William Barnard, Bishop of Raphoe and Derry lived there. After his death in 1768 it was bought by a London impressario, who turned the house and gardens into an entertainment area, complete with theatre and teahouse. The residence was renamed Ranelagh after the fashionable Ranelagh Gardens in London and the name was quickly adopted by the whole area. An English writer visiting the gardens in 1781 witnessed "A curious exhibition of fireworks. The temple was particularly beautiful. The music in different parts of the garden and a most delightful effect, particularly that which came from a tree, half a dozen musicans being placed among the branches."

In 1785 Ireland's first aeronaut, Richard Crosbie made a balloon ascent from the entertainment gardens. In the last century the gardens fate was more prosaic with the Carmelite convent of St Joseph's being built in the grounds. The nuns did, however, run a free school for the local girls.

The district's most distinguished resident during the 18th century was Dr Bartholomew Mosse. Born in Marybor-ough in 1712, he became famous internationally as an expert in surgery and midwifery. Appalled at the suffering of poor women in Dublin he opened the first maternity hospital in these islands at a house in George's Lane, off South Great George's Street, on March 14th, 1745. He gave his own services free to the poor and raised funds by lotteries, concerts and public subscriptions. He also advised on the establishment of London's first maternity hospital, which was modelled on his own.

During the early 19th century Ranelagh grew rapidly, like neighbouring Rathmines. In the ten years from 1821 to 1831 alone the population rose from 913 to 1,988.

William Edward Hartpole Lecky, the eminent Irish historian, was born at Cullenswood House, Ranelagh, in 1838. His 'History of Ireland in the Eighteenth Century' is a classic of historical literature. Incidentally Padraic Pearse set up St Enda's College at Cullenswood House before moving to Rathfarnham.

The infamous Major Sirr once resided at Elm Park, Ranelagh, but when his wife died he retired to Dublin Castle, where he died in 1841 aged 82. Padraic Colum, the poet and dramatist once lived in Edenvale Road.

Trinity House in Charleston Road was a former Methodist church which was converted to office use in 1983. The building was redesigned by architect Reg Chandler for McInerney's and won the Dublin Corporation's overall cultural and environmental award for 1983.

(Continued from Page 8)

mile cycle championship in Copenhagen. Shortly afterwards he turned professional and went on a world tour, visiting Tasmania, New Zealand and the USA. A most remarkable feature of his career is that, after retiring in 1901, he made a comeback in 1906, winning the National Cycling Union professional championship that year. Known as 'The Balbriggan Flyer' he continued to compete for a number of years and was renowned for his powers of endurance and grit.

Hampton Hall, the fine mansion built by the Hamilton family in 1758, was burned to the ground on a Tuesday evening, May 14th, 1901. The house

Balbriggan

was situated near the sea, a short distance from Balbriggan and today Colaiste Phadraig stands on the site.

Balbriggan was 'sacked' during the War of Independence by a force of Black and Tans from nearby Gormanstown Camp, on Monday September 20th,

1920. It was a reprisal raid for the killing of Detective Inspector Peter Burke of the RIC. Burke was shot dead and another man wounded during a quarrel in a local bar, allegedly with the IRA. Twenty-five houses, many of them thatched, and a small factory were burnt out that night. The terrified inhabitants fled into the fields to escape the drink crazed Tans. Several republicans were arrested and two young men, Seamus Lawless and John Gibbons, were later found dead, bayoneted in the street. The incident generated much sympathy abroad for the Irish cause, particularly in America, where a commission was set up to investigate the outrages being committed in Ireland.

RANELAGH
CULLENSWOOD

ON EASTER MONDAY 1209 CULLENSWOOD (NOW RANELAGH) WAS THE SCENE OF THE MASSACRE OF 500 BRISTOLIAN SETTLERS BY THE WICKLOW MOUNTAIN SEPTS.

WLM. E.H. LECKY THE EMINENT IRISH HISTORIAN WAS BORN AT CULLENSWOOD HOUSE IN 1838

THE FIRST BALLOON ASCENT IN IRELAND WAS MADE ON JANUARY THE 19TH 1785 FROM RANELAGH GARDENS, DUBLIN.

JWREN

Rathfarnham

Rath Farnan   (Farnan's Fort)

Rathfarnham (Farnan's Rath), like Raheny on the north side of Dublin, takes its name from the rath or fort of some long forgotten celtic headman or chieftan named Farnan. Shortly after the Anglo-Norman invasion the lands of Rathfarnham came into the possession of Milo De Brett in 1199 and his descendants retained ownership of these lands for many generations.

In the late 15th century Geoffrey Le Bret of Rathfarnham gained such a reputation as a warrior in the fight against native Irish that the English king summoned him to assist him in his war against the French and later against the Scots. The great Danish Harold family, after whom Harolds Cross is called, were for a long period tenants of the Bretts of Rathfarnham, as were the Archibalds and the Walshs.

The Harolds remained chief tenants here until the 15th century when Rathfarnham passed from the Brets to the Eustace family of Baltinglass. In 1585 Elizabeth I of England granted the confiscated estate of James Eustace, 3rd Viscount Baltinglass, who had fought in the Desmond rebellion, to Adam Loftus the Protestant Archbishop of Dublin.

Adam Loftus, who was made Lord High Chancellor in 1578, was one of the principal founders of Trinity College, Dublin, where he became first Provost. On the site of the original castle at Rathfarnham Archbishop Loftus erected the present building and came to reside here in 1585.

Loftus was born in Yorkshire and came to Ireland with the Earl of Sussex. After some time as the Archbishop of Armagh he was appointed to the See of Dublin, which he held for 37 years. During a period of great religious persecution in Ireland, Loftus as Lord Justice was responsible for torturing and executing Dr. Dermott O'Hurley, the Catholic Archbishop of Cashel.

When Archbishop Loftus died at the age of 72, in 1605, he was succeeded at Rathfarnham by his eldest son Sir Dudley Loftus who, in turn, was followed by his son Sir Adam Loftus. Sir Adam Loftus was a politician who was on friendly terms with all the leading and distinguished people in the Ireland of his day particularly the great Earl of Cork.

In 1641 Rathfarnham Castle was garrisoned under the command of Dudley Loftus who had just returned from his Oxford studies and defended from the attack of the rebel forces. During this period a Henry Butterfield of Rathfarnham was robbed by the rebels and taken to Powerscourt where he was hanged, the modern townland of Butterfield is called after him.

In July 1649 Rathfarnham Castle was garrisoned by a force of Parliamentarians, who were overrun by Royalists a few days before the Battle of Rathmines, without the loss of a single life. Adam Loftus the son of Sir Adam died at the siege of Limerick when he was hit by a cannon ball in September 1691. He had been created a peer by James II in 1686 but served as a Colonel of a foot regiment in the Irish army of William of Orange during the subsequent hostilities.

The Castle of Rathfarnham passed by marriage to the Marquis of Wharton in 1723 and William Connolly the speaker of the Irish House of Commons later became its owner. In 1767 Rathfarnham was purchased by the 2nd Earl of Ely, a descendant of Archbishop Loftus, so it reverted to the original family owners.

In 1771 the famous artist Angelia Kauffmann, while on an Irish visit, painted the panels of the drawing room ceiling for the Elys. In 1913 Rathfarnham castle became the property of the Society of Jesus, who made extensive alterations. "Cromwells Barn", which now forms part of the retreat house, was believed to have been used by Oliver Cromwell as a council room during his Irish campaign.

The imposing 18th century mansion which forms the centre position of the buildings of Loretto Abbey, Rathfarnham, was built by William Palliser, the wealthy son of the Archbishop of Cashel. John Grierson, the King's Printer, lived here at the time of the Union and, in 1822, the Loretto nuns established their headquarters in this house. Near Loretto Abbey stands the crumbling ruin of the Priory, which was once the home of the celebrated lawyer, John Philpot Curran, father of Sarah Curran, Robert Emmet's fiance.

About a mile from the village is the Pearse Museum at Saint Enda's, where Patrick Pearse founded his Irish speaking school, in 1910, in the fine old georgian mansion which was built by the Hodson family and was formerly called the "Hermitage". Here in the grounds there is a tree-lined path called "Emmet's Walk". Here it is said that the great Irish patriot used to walk with Sarah Curran in the shadow of the Dublin foothills.

BRIDGE AT RATHFARNHAM

RATHFARNHAM FARNANS FORT

RATHFARNHAM, LYING IN THE SHADOW OF THE DUBLIN HILLS HOLDS MANY MEMORIES OF ROBERT EMMET AND THE RISING OF 1803. IT WAS HERE HE MET SARAH CURRAN IN HER FATHER'S HOUSE "THE PRIORY."

ENTRANCE HALL RATHFARNHAM CASTLE

RATHFARNHAM CASTLE

ADAM LOFTUS BUILDER OF RATHFARNHAM CASTLE

IN 1910 PATRICK PEARSE MOVED HIS SCHOOL ST. ENDA'S INTO A FINE OLD GEORGIAN MANSION "THE HERMITAGE" AT RATHFARNHAM. IT IS NOW A MUSEUM AND THE GROUNDS ARE NOW A PUBLIC PARK.

Rathgar

The translation of the name Rathgar is given as Rath Gharbh, or the rough ring fort, but it is uncertain where this ancient site was. Henderson, writing in 1914, believed it stood near Rathgar Castle (Rathgar Lodge is now on the site) because at that time there was a low rounded mound to the rere of the houses on Templemore Road, and it may have stood here.

The lands of Rathgar were, in the middle ages, the grange or home farm of the Abbey of St Mary de Hogges – a convent of Augustinian nuns who lived on what later became College Green, but was then known as The Hogges or mounds.

The farm was renowned for its wealth and extensive granary and outbuildings. A David Lugg was sentenced to death in the 14th century for theft from the farm buildings. There were also extensive woodlands. The general area was part of the parish of St Nicholas Without, which included Cullenswood, St Kevin's and areas of the mediaeval city "without the walls".

For some years prior to the Reformation the lands were leased to James Richards, but afterwards they were granted by the crown to Nicholas Segrave (see Cabra). At the beginning of the 17th century Rathgar came into the possession of another wellknown Dublin family, the Cusacks. John Cusack, a leading merchant and Lord Mayor of Dublin in 1608, was the first resident here. His son Robert succeeded him and was Sheriff for the County of Dublin during the great rebellion of the 1640s.

His property was severely damaged during the period. Corn, horses and carts were commandeered by royalist troops and, after the battle of Rathmines, many of these soldiers took refuge in Cusack's house and the neighbouring woods. After a parley the royalists agreed to surrender on being promised their lives and many of them promptly joined the victorious Cromwellian forces.

Being Protestants, the Cusacks were permitted to retain their estates although they had supported the defeated King. Rathgar took a long time to recover from the ravages of war. At the time of the restoration the total population consisted of the Cusack family of John, his wife Alice, and their children John and Katherine, plus two man servants and two women servants. The only other inhabitants were two destitute women.

The Cusack family continued to live in Rathgar well into the 18th century. Amongst the owners of the estate were Adam Cusack, who became Chief Justice of the Provincial Court of Connaught and was appointed to the Court of Common Pleas. He was related by marriage to both the Lord Chancellor, Sir Maurice Eustace and the Chief Justice of Common Pleas, John Keatinge. On

his death he bequeathed substantial sums to the poor of Rathfarnham and the hospitals at Back Lane and Oxmantown. His wife, a daughter of John Keatinge, later Adam's brother, Nicholas Cusack. The lands were nearly lost to The lands were nearly lost to the family when he was accused of treason in 1690 but subsequently he was pardoned.

During the 18th century the estate gradually fell into disrepair and only the walls and gateway entrance remained standing. The lands were let out to market gardeners and dairymen. The area was a haunt of highwaymen and one of the sons of a local farmer, John Mooney, was hanged for highway robbery. His life was later the theme of a popular religious tract of the period.

Settlement of the area by Dubliners only began in 1753 when Chief Justice Yorke had a roadway constructed from his residence at Rathmines Castle to Terenure. This is now Highfield Road. By 1784 the old Cusack estate was so dilapidated that it was used for manouevres, complete with a sham battle and siege, by the Irish Volunteers. It was only with the rapid growth of Rathmines in the nineteenth century that Rathgar too developed into a middle class suburb of the city. Several Georgian houses in Rathgar bear testimony to its once rural and wooded terrain, such as Highfield, Ashgrove and Oaklands.

In 1837 there was an extensive bleach green with a printing works at Rathgar and this was set in motion by a 30 hp and a water wheel. Here Messrs Waldron, Dodd and Carter & Co. manufactured muslin, calicoes and silks and employed a workforce of 300 men. Rathgar also possessed quarries of good limestone and black calp which were extensively worked in the 18th and 19th centuries.

The Catholic church of the Three Patrons on Rathgar Road was opened in 1862 as a chapel of ease to Rathmines. In 1882, when Rathgar was constituted a separate parish, the new parish priest appointed was a historian, the Very Rev Dr Nicholas Donnelly, the Bishop of Canea and author of 'A Short History of Dublin Parishes'. Dr Donnelly was familiar with the area since his childhood and attended "a sort of secondary school" at Harold's Cross in 1850. He left Rathgar in 1894 to take charge of Bray parish.

Christ Church, the handsome Presbyterian building which stands at the junction where the five roads meet in Rathgar village, was opened on November 2nd, 1859. In February 1874 the foundation stone for the Methodist church at Brighton Road was laid. This edifice in the early English style was designed by Thomas Holbrook, CE. The Church of Ireland building of the Zion Parish, Rathgar, was completed in 1862 and was considered at the time to be one of the best specimens of ecclesiastical architecture in the city, or suburbs. The material used included calp and granite for the rubble walling, Portland stone for the cut stone dressings and Caen stone for the internal columns. Thomas Welland and Sons were responsible for the design of this fine building.

A number of wellknown people from the world of literature and art have resided in the area over the last 100 years. The poet and painter 'AE', George Russell, lived at 17 Rathgar Avenue from 1906 to 1933. His family's first Dublin address was at 33 Emorville Avenue and he attended Doctor Benson's school in Rathmines Road between 1882 and 1884. James Joyce was born in 41 Brighton Square, Rathgar in 1882 and moved with his parents to 23 Castlewood Avenue in 1885.

William Carleton, the author of many books on 19th century Irish peasant life, moved to 1 Rathgar Avenue from Clontarf in 1853 and lived there for many years. Another northsider, Bram Stoker, settled in 5 Orwell Park after living in Artane Lodge as a boy. The house next door, 4 Orwell Park, was the home of John Millington Synge from 1871 to 1890. From this house the solitary Synge made many excursions into the Dublin mountains and Wicklow glens in his teens.

Joseph Robinson Kirk RHA, the son of Scots born Thomas Kirk RHA, lived on Rathgar Road in the 1860s. Kirk was one of the foremost Irish sculptors of the 19th century and his work included the Seringapatam Panel on the Wellington Memorial, the sculptured representation of a military troiphy in Forster Place and the Crampton Memorial which once stood at the junction of College Street and D'Olier Street.

RATHGAR

THE LANDS OF RATHGAR WERE IN MEDIAEVAL TIMES THE GRANGE OR FARM LANDS OF THE CONVENT OF ST. MARY DE HOGGES, COLLEGE GREEN.

RATHGAR QUARRY AND WINDMILL IN THE 18TH CENTURY

AFTER THE BATTLE OF RATHMINES A LARGE, BODY OF LORD INCHIQUIN'S SOLDIERY TOOK REFUGE IN THE GROVES OF RATHGAR.

FAMOUS WRITERS AND RATHGAR

JAMES JOYCE   BRAM STOKER   WILL CARLETON   GEORGE RUSSELL (AE)

Rathmines

The district of Rathmines derives its name from the de Meones family, who accompanied Archbishop de Derlington to Dublin from Hampshire, on his elevation to the archbishopric in 1279.

The best known member of the family to occupy a fort, or rath in the area was Gilbert de Meones, a soldier who held the lands from the archbishop as part of the Manor of St Sepulchre. Other members of the family held high civil and ecclesiastical office in Dublin. The family also held lands around what is now Mount Argus and Harold's Cross. A successor of Gilbert, William de Meones, was the first member of the family to describe himself as Lord of Meones' Rath.

Before that the arrival of the de Meones' family the lands had been held by Richard de Welton and were part of the parish of St Kevin, which included a section of the old city as well as farmland beyond the walls.

Built as a defensive post for the city against the raiding Wicklow septs, the village of Rathmines gradually developed around the fort and a mill was built on the river Dodder, nearby by the de Meones.

In the 1630s Sir George Radcliffe, a favourite of the Viceroy, Lord Strafford, acquired the lands and built a house for £7,000 on the present site of Palmerston Park, Strafford was a regular visitor to the house and probably engaged in his favourite pastime of falconry when there. He was recalled in disgrace, with Strafford and imprisoned while Strafford himself was executed for treason in May 1642. In October of the same year the Great Rebellion broke out in Ulster. It rapidly spread to the rest of the country and the Earl of Ormonde was appointed viceroy to deal with the rebels by King Charles I. Ormonde used Radcliffe's new house to accommodate his family but, due to the disturbed state of the country, he withdrew them inside the city walls. The house was burned by rebels shortly afterwards.

Rathmines continued to be used as a base to harry Dublin by the rebel forces through the 1640s. In 1649 there was a curious reversal of roles, when Ormonde joined the rebels to attack the city. It was now held by Colonel Michael Jones for the English republican forces, their last outpost in the country.

The new alliance of rebels and royalists besieged the city with a force of 11,500, most of whom were concentrated around Rathmines. Early on August 2nd, 1649, Ormonde's forces attempted a surprise attack on a parliamentary outpost at Baggotrath castle, near the present site of Baggot Street bridge. Jones retaliated with a fullscale counterattack, after drawing up his 6,000 troops in formation on meadowland running from the present day Merrion Square to where the banks of the Grand Canal now stand. Thrusting through Ranelagh ans supported by a flanking attack through Donnybrook, Jones's highly disciplined Roundheads soon put the rebels to flight. A few rebels took refuge in nearby Cullenswood and were massacred when they surrendered.

Thirteen days after the battle Oliver Cromwell arrived in Ireland and began its systematic reconquest. He described Jones's victory as "an astonishing mercy, so great and seasonable that we are like them that dreamed".

During Cromwell's Commonwealth, Radcliffe House was restored and occupied by a Captain Shore, one of his officers. The ravages of war had reduced the population of the area however, to six Irish and six English persons. When Shore died in 1668 the property was disputed for many years by his heirs and those of his predecessor, Sir George Radcliffe. In the early eighteenth century the estate came into the possession of the Temple family, which took the name of Palmerston, another of its Irish estates when ennobled. The most famous member of the family was Lord Palmerston, British prime minister in the mid-nineteenth century.

During the eighteenth century the population of Rathmines rapidly grew and reached 1,600 by the 1830s. The common at the centre of the old village was reduced to a small triangle of land, which still stands at the junction of Upper and Lower Rathmines Road. In the mid-eighteenth century Rathmines and Rathgar were linked for the first time by the construction of what is now Highfield Road.

By 1823 Rathmines was large enough to become an independent parish and its first Catholic church was opened by Archbishop Murray in August 1830. By 1848 it was decided to build a second church for what was now Dublin's largest suburb and the first stone of the Memorial Church of Definition of the Dogma of the Immaculate Conception of the Blessed Virgin was laid in 1850. It was opened by Cardinal Cullen in 1856 and is one of the finest examples of ecclesiastical architecture in these islands. The building was badly gutted by fire in January 1920, but was completely restored.

Rathmines became one of the country's first urban district council areas after the passing of the Municipal Reform Act in 1840. The town commissioners decided to build a large town hall (1887) that would also serve as a social centre for the community and the result was the impressive building now standing on the Rathmines Road, designed by Sir Thomas Drew. Its most distinctive feature is the clock tower. The clock itself cost £164 10s and has been notoriously unreliable over the years, earning it the reputation of a 'four faced liar' by local wags.

In 1896 Marconi demonstrated his wireless telegraphy invention there and one of Eddison's first movie films was shown in 1902 at the town hall. In 1899 Percy French performed there. During the War of Independence the building was taken over by the British Army.

During this period one of the area's most interesting residents was Constance Markiewicz, the first woman elected to the House of Commons and the first woman to hold ministerial office in any government in these islands, when she served as Minister for Labour in the First Dáil. She lived at Surray House, 49b Leinster Road, from 1912 to 1916, when British soldiers wrecked and looted the premises during the Easter Rising. They also uncovered an illegal printing press used to produce anti-recruiting and other subversive literature. After her release from prison Constance Markiewicz moved to Frankfort House nearby, where she stayed with Dr Kathleen Lynn and the Coughlin family.

Like the smaller Pembroke urban district council, Rathmines fell a victim of the Local Government (Dublin) Act of 1930. It was abolished and the 100,000 population of the two councils were absorbed into the Dublin Corporation area. The town hall is now part of the City of Dublin's Vocational Education Committee premises.

To the rere of the elegant Mount Pleasant Square, which dates to the 1740s, the Mount Pleasant flats complex was built by Rathmines UDC in 1901 to provide accommodation for workers and their families. Over the years the complex became dilapidated and was eventually demolished a decade ago. Lee Dunne, the author of 'Goodbye to the Hill', spent his younger days in Mount Pleasant buildings and recorded his experiences in the novel.

Ringsend and Irishtown

Roinn Aun   (Seapoint)

Ringsend, or the end of the Point, was an uninhabited place until the 17th century, when it replaced Dalkey as the port of Dublin. Ringsend was the chief place of embarkation and disembarkation between the 17th and 19th centuries for cross-channel passengers. This trade ceased when Howth and later Dun Laoghaire harbours were built.

In 1620 a station house was built at Ringsend for Thomas Cave, a revenue surveyor, and by 1660 there were 59 persons of English and 21 of Irish descent living there. At that time Ringsend, which was almost surrounded by water, was a very busy village. Nearby lay a wood between Irishtown and Beggars Bush which, we are told was "a resort of robbers".

In 1647 there landed and camped at Ringsend an English Parliamentary force under Colonel Michael Jones, who had crossed the Irish sea to negotiate Dublin's surrender by the Royalist Duke of Ormonde. Ormonde handed over the city to Jones, a move he later regretted. In 1649 he laid siege to the city, but his forces were defeated by Jones in the battle of Rathmines. Before the battle a company of Parliamentarians, who were stationed at Ringsend, were attacked and defeated by a detatchment of Royalists from Ormonde's camp at Finglas. When Oliver Cromwell landed at Ringsend on 18th August 1649 with a well equipped army of 12,000 men, he was welcomed by the city fathers of Dublin, which was by then firmly under the control of the English Parliament. From the forts and the ships that were anchored in the Liffey cannon boomed while bells in the city peeled and the streets were decorated with flags and bunting.

In 1690 James II rode out to Ringsend to witness a naval engagement between several vessels under the command of Sir Cloudesley Shovel and one of his own frigates laden with goods for France. There have been a number of historical references to a well known tavern at Ringsend called "The Kings Head". In 1683 a notorious family of bandits, the Brennans, laid low for some days at this tavern and escaped with property valued at £12,000. John Dunton, writing in 1699, said they were "nobly treated at the King's Head, at this dear place".

In 1707, when a ballast office was founded, operations began in clearing and widening the channel into Dublin port for shipping. In 1711 the Liffey was embanked between the city and Ringsend. The great South Wall, one of the most outstanding achievements of marine engineering in the world, was commenced in 1714 and finally completed in 1796. Originally a framework of wooden piling, it was replaced in 1735 by a double stone wall. The intervening space was filled with boulders and gravel, forming a roadway.

The Poolbeg lighthouse, at the furthest extremity of the South Wall, was opened on 29th September 1767 and was the first lighthouse in the world to use candles. All other lighthouses up to that time used coals. The name, the Pidgeon House, was derived from a strongly built wooden house, which was erected on the South Wall during its own construction for the use of the overseer and caretaker. His name was John Pidgeon.

In time Pidgeon's house became a hostelry, and he and his family supplemented their incomes by running boat trips around the bay, a business which the old man's daughters carried on after his death. When a cross channel packet station and a harbour was established here, a hotel was built at the Pidgeon House in 1790, for the accommodation of travellers. In 1814 the government erected a fort here and, in 1843, it was the guns of the Pidgeon House Fort which were trained on the Clontarf Road to Conquer Hill, where O'Connell's monster repeal meeting was to take place. The Pidgeon House has been used for many purposes since 1790, including a store for state papers, and is today the offices of the E.S.B. generating station.

From the Ancient Calendar of the Records of Dublin, in the year 1454, we find a decree of the Corporation ordering all people of Irishblood to quit the city within four weeks under the threat of imprisonment on refusing to obey the order. These homeless victims, both clergy and lay people, made their way eastward to the seashore where they established a community at what became known as Irishtown.

Saint Matthew's church, Irishtown, which was built in 1703 for Protestant seamen, has a fine bellfry and it is believed that the vaults were once used by smugglers because of its then isolated position. In 1790 Theobold Wolfe Tone rented a little seaside house at Irishtown and, in his memoirs, he recalls many happy days spent there. A regular visitor was Thomas Russell, who was later hanged for his part in Robert Emmet's rebellion. In the 18th century Irishtown was one of the popular Dublin venues where hurling games were played and there is a record of a game held here in 1757 between married men and batchelors for a wager of 50 guineas a side. Unfortunately, the result is not recorded.

RINGSEND BRIDGE

RINGSEND

OLIVER CROMWELL WHO HAD BEEN APPOINTED LORD LIEUTENANT OF IRELAND LANDED AT RINGSEND IN AUGUST 1649 WITH AN ARMY OF 12000 MEN

POOLBEG LIGHTHOUSE

THE PIGEON HOUSE TAKES ITS NAME FROM A JOHN PIDGEON WHO KEPT A HOSTELRY ON THE GREAT SOUTH WALL DURING THE TIME OF ITS CONSTRUCTION.

RAHENY

(Continued from Page 72)

The Raheny Inn was opened as a public house in 1959 and stands on the site of an older inn and another building which was the venue for the Raheny petty sessions during the last century. The village also held a forge until recent times and the Crowe family were blacksmiths there for several generations. A pharmacy now occupies the site, which is a few doors away from the Village Inn.

Another vanished landmark is Raheny Park. Built by Thomas Gresham (founder of the Gresham Hotel), it stood half way between the fillage and the Old Sheiling Hotel. This house was occupied by the Dollards, a well-known printing family, at the end of the last century.

They were followed by Stephen Gwynne MP, a leading member of the Irish Parliamentary Party. Visitors to the house included John Redmond, Patrick Pearse, Roger Casement, Tom Kettle and the poet James Stephens.

In more recent times church building has provided Raheny with its most prominent structure. The modern church of Our Lady, Mother of Divine Grace, replaces the old Catholic church of St. Assam's which stands across the Howth Road opposite the new building.

Unlike the other St. Assam's (now a ruin), the former Catholic parish church serves as a community hall. It was designed by Patrick Byrne, the leading church architect of his day, and was opened in 1864.

The new church provides a striking example of modern celtic architecture and has a triangular front based on the Hiberno-Romanesque style. The idea for the door motif was based on the splendid carvings of the west door of the ancient cathedral of Clonfert, Co. Galway. The architects for the new church were Peppard and Duffy.

Returning to Raheny's older buildings, it is not generally known that to the rere of the Manhattan Bar stood Rathmore House, the home of the Sweetman family for many years. Brewers in the city, the Sweetmans also played a distinguished role in Irish politics.

It was about 1810 that William Sweetman came to reside here. He had a brewery at Aston's Quay. Another member of the family, John Sweetman, designed the Pro-Cathedral. He submitted his design for the cathedral from Paris because he had been exiled for his involvement in the United Irishmen.

Beside the Manhattan Bar is a neat little crescent of cottages dating back 200 years. Originally built to house servants and tenants of Edenmore House, one of them caused a mild sensation recently on being sold for £17,000. The weekly rent previously for this little four roomed dwelling was 45p a week.

Walmer House is situated just beyond the cottages, and St. Vincent's GAA grounds on Grange Road. In the 1840s it was the home of Captain William Bryan, a leading Young Irelander.

A shadowy figure, Bryan made his fortune as a squatter in Tasmania. His home at Raheny was the venue for many a Saturday night social gathering. John Mitchel said of Bryan that he was a gruff but kindly old gentleman, always in a state of sustained indignation against England and everything English.

Belmont House, the Capuchin Hostel which also stands on Grange Road, is in the townland of Mount Olive where, in the 18th century, Benjamin Pemberton operated a large windmill. The land of Raheny and Kilbarrack was, at that time, one huge granary.

In the 18th and 19th centuries the limestone quarries of Raheny were also worked extensively. "Falkner's Journal" reported the discovery of an underground cavern there where the walls were found to contain primitive drawings of human and animal forms. Unfortunately these were never preserved.

Finally Edenmore House, a magnificent early Georgian building still stands near the village. It dates from the first half of the 18th century but, unfortunately, its builder is unknown.

In 1878 Samuel Dick, a wealthy Dublin merchant of Linenhall Street, came to live at Violet Hill, as Edenmore House was then called. A governor of the Bank of Ireland, Mr. Dick donated the site on Station Road where the eight Crescent Cottages now stand.

In 1839, when Dublin's Lord Mayor George Hoyte was in residence at Edenmore House, the Dublin-Drogheda railway was opened. In March 1844 a special train, on its return journey from Drogheda stopped at Raheny station and the passenger guests, led by the Lord Lieutenant, adjourned to Edenmore House to be entertained with a banquet and ball by Hoyte.

Perhaps because of its proximity to the railway, Patrick Moore of Moore Brothers Railway Architects, lived here for a number of years. He was followed by John Maunsell, solicitor of the Dublin Metropolitan Police.

In 1958 the Sisters of St. Joseph of Chambry purchased the mansion and converted it into the 68 bed private hospital of St. Joseph which it is today.

DR. HAYES MEMORIAL, RAHENY

IRISH TOWN

ACCORDING TO THE ANCIENT RECORDS OF DUBLIN THE CORPORATION ISSUED A DECREE IN 1454 ORDERING ALL MEN AND WOMEN OF IRISH BLOOD WHETHER NUNS, CLERICS, JOURNEYMEN, APPRENTICES, SERVANTS, BEGGARS, ETC., "TO QUIT THE CITY WITHIN FOUR WEEKS, AND ANYONE FOUND WITHIN THE CITY GATES AFTER THAT TIME SHALL FORFEIT THEIR GOODS, CHATELS, ETC., AND BE CAST INTO PRISON AND SUFFER OTHER PENALTIES."

THESE PEOPLE SETTLED ON THE SPOT OUTSIDE THE CITY WHICH IS KNOWN TODAY AS IRISHTOWN

IT IS BELIEVED THAT THE VAULTS OF ST. MATTHEW'S CHURCH IRISHTOWN WERE USED AS A SMUGGLERS LAIR DURING THE EIGHTEENTH CENT.

IRISHTOWN GREEN IN THE 18TH. CENTURY WAS THE VENUE FOR MANY HURLING GAMES AND ON 29TH. SEPT. 1757 A MATCH BETWEEN A TEAM OF MARRIED MEN AND ONE OF BATCHELORS FOR A WAGER OF 50 GUINEAS A SIDE WAS PLAYED

IN THE SUMMER OF 1790 THEOBOLD WOLFE TONE TOOK A SMALL COTTAGE AT IRISHTOWN. HE SPENT SOME HAPPY MONTHS WITH HIS FAMILY THERE.

Rush

Ros Eo

(the headland of yew trees)

The Gaelic name of Ros Eo for Rush recalls the widespread growth of this evergreen in Ireland during early times. Another local name is Kenure or Ceann Lubair, meaning the head of yews.

The little ruined church of Kenure standing close to the Rush-Skerries road occupies the site of a Celtic foundation originally dedicated to Saint Damnan. The 7th century holy man Saint Cuanne was also connected with Rush and the chapel at Kenure was later dedicated to Saint Catherine. A well in the nearby estate was called after her. The ruin measures 52 feet by 22 and contains a number of old tombs and the remains of several parish priests who lived in the 18th century are buried here.

On the Dublin side of Rush another old church dedicated to the French saint, Maur, stands at Whitestown. According to local legend a party of French crusaders returning from the Holy Land were driven by storm into the shelter of Rogerstown Haven. At the height of the tempest the crusaders vowed to build a church to St Maur wherever they landed if their lives were spared. The church was erected a little inland from the estuary and dedicated to the much venerated French saint. The place was known initially as Knightstown but with the passing of time it changed to Whitestown.

From the reign of Edward I until 1641 the lands of Rush were in the possession of the House of Ormond. When the Duke then fell from favour they passed to the Echlin family. In the mid-18th century the Echlins lost Kenure and their other properties and Roger Palmer of Castlelaken, Co Mayo, bought the Rush lands.

Palmer's wife, Eleanor Ambrose, was a prominent socialite. During the vice royalty of the Fourth Earl of Chesterfield from 1945 to 1747 she, and her sister Clara of Mount Ambrose, County Dublin, were among the great beauties of the Castle set. Chesterfield was attracted by Eleanor's beauty and quick wit and she accompanied him to all his official ceremonies.

Later, while discussing Ireland with King George II, Chesterfield said it was poverty, not popery that was to be feared in Ireland. He had found "only one dangerous Papist there and she was a beautiful young lady, the brightness of whose eyes and charms of whose conversation were indeed dangerous and her name was Eleanor Ambrose." She lived to be 98 and died in her house at Henry Street, Dublin in 1818. There she kept a portrait of the former viceroy, who she regarded as the only Englishman who sympathised with the sufferings of her co-religionists.

Eleanor Ambrose married Sir Roger Palmer, the First Baronet. A descendant was Lieutenant General Sir Roger Palmer, the third baronet, who died in 1910 and was one of the last surviving officers of the Charge of the Light Brigade at Balaclave in the Crimean War, which was immortalised in Tennyson's poem. Palmer was a lieutenant in the 11th Hussars at the time and, according to the historian Kingslake's account of the action Palmer captured a high ranking Russian officer, who surrendered his sword to him. On another occasion Sir Roger alerted his comrades to an approaching Russian force. All that remains today of the old mansion however is the 19th century portico which was added by the architect George Papworth.

Around the district of Rush and along the coast of Fingal many families are descended from the hardy Norse sea rovers who settled here in the 9th and 10th centuries. It is not surprising therefore that for hundreds of years Rush was a notable fishing port.

The lot of 18th century fishermen was hazardous and poor. For this reason many were also smugglers, attracted by the profits and excitement. The little port of Rogerstown between Rush and Portrane was a busy unloading spot for contraband, including brandy, rum and tea, which were then known as 'run goods'. Almost the entire population of Rush and Portrane were involved in smuggling and in 1777 over 500 fully armed smugglers attacked a party of revenue officers guarding seized goods at Portrane. Rush smuggler, Captain Luke Ryan sailed as a privateer under American and French flags.

In April 1781, while sailing under a French commission, Captain Ryan and his crew were finally captured by an English man-o-war off the Scottish coast. He was given a pardon after the intercession of the French court during peace negotiations. He was not released however, but died in prison after serving six years as a debtor in the King's Bench prison.

Another famous Rush smuggler was Jack 'The Batchelor' Connor, who was born in Wexford. His colourful career began when he was a youngster involved in the smuggling trade between Rush, the Isle of Man and later Dunkirk. On several occasions he engaged with the Revenue cutters but always escaped capture.

He gained a reputation in north county Dublin as a Robin Hood figure and many stories circulated of his generosity to the poor. Along with his boon companion, Captain Fields of Rush, he sailed 'run goods' into the area for two decades until his sudden death in 1772 aged only 36. His burial at Kenure was attended by a huge gathering and the grave of Jack the Batchelor overlooks the coastline of Fingal from the little churchyard.

John Murphy, a Rush born smuggler lived to die of old age in the seaport of Nantes in 1837. No seaman knew better than he the Irish coast, the English Channel and the shores of France. In 1798 they found him in Killala Bay when the French general, Humbert, landed with his forces. Murphy offered his services to the French commander and ran the gauntlet of British warships with despatches to France. In recognition of his services he was presented with a brace of pistols by the French directory and promoted to the rank of pilot to the French fleet at Brest. In 1814, when the Bourbons were returned to power, he returned to the mercantile marine to support his wife and six children still living in Ireland. He was given command of a fine ship by a wealthy Nantes merchant and sailed the world's trade routes.

In 1823, while in command of a French whaler, his crew mutinied. Murphy, his first lieutenant and mate were clapped in irons. After a fortnight the mutineers failed to reach sanctuary in Spain and the mate was forced to steer. He led them into French waters and a French naval sloop recaptured the vessel, rescuing the imprisoned officers. The sailors were condemned to imprisonment in the galleys.

Amongst other wellknown and skilful Rush captains who engaged in smuggling were Thomas and Joseph Richard, Patrick Dowling, John Kelly alias Grumley, Robert Burnat and John McCarthy.

The present parish church of St Maur in Rush, which is under imminent threat of destruction to make way for a more 'modern' building, was modelled on its predecessor by the great church architect, George Ashlin. The earlier distinguished building was erected in 1760.

Today Rush is noted for its market gardening and acres of green houses and retains the old world charm with thatched houses still to be seen in the village streets.

RUSH

THERE IS A LEGEND THAT A PARTY OF FRENCH CRUSADER KNIGHTS WHEN DRIVEN OFF COURSE THROUGH TEMPEST LANDED SAFELY IN ROGERSTOWN HAVEN. IN THANKSGIVING FOR THEIR ESCAPE THEY BUILT A CHURCH AT WHITESTOWN AND DEDICATED IT TO THE FRENCH SAINT MAUR.

KENURE PARK, RUSH WAS FOR TWO CENTURIES THE HOME OF THE PALMER FAMILY UNTIL 1978 WHEN IT WAS DEMOLISHED. SIR ROGER PALMER WHO DIED IN 1910 WAS ONE OF THE FEW SURVIVORS OF THE CHARGE OF THE LIGHT BRIGADE AT BALAKLAVA.

SMUGGLERS WERE ONCE VERY ACTIVE IN THE RUSH AREA AND JACK CONNOR (JACK THE BACHELOR) HAD A WIDE REPUTATION IN THE 18TH CENTURY.

JWREN

Sandymount
Scallet Hill

This was one of Dublin's smallest villages, wedged between the Simmonscourt estate to the east and the sea to the west. Its early name was Scalled Hill or Scallett Hill. As late as the 16th century its main feature was a large rabbit warren built on this rise, which was covered in furze.

Its first recorded landlord was Richard de St Olof in the 13th century. He also owned the richer lands of Simmonscourt. They later passed through the hands of the Bagods and FitzWilliams into the possession of the Priory of the Holy Trinity and then back to the FitzWilliams of Merrion again.

Sandymount's chief asset was the rough pasture and fishing centre. Much of it was low lying and had become salt marshes. The herring fishery ran along the coast here from Merrion to Ringsend. The fish were highly regarded and considered superior to any other herrings in these islands. A toll of 500 choice herring was levied each year by the FitzWilliams on the fishery.

Early in the eighteenth century the soil was found suitable for making bricks and the area became known as Lord Merrion's brickfields. A village called Brickfield Town sprang up and its most famous structure was a thatched inn called The Conniving House. Run by Johnny Macklean, it was renowned for its fish dinners and ale. At the beginning of the 19th century several Martello towers were built along the seafront during the Napoleonic wars. One of these is still standing and serves as a cafe.

Over the next 100 years the area became an agreeable retreat for the city's middle classes and developers changed its name to Sandymount to enhance its appeal. By the mid-century the present village had assumed its present form, taking shape around the triangular square.

James Gandon, the great architect of Dublin's Custom House designed Sandymount Park towards the end of the 18th century. Its first owner was William Ashford, an English born artist who exhibited with the Society of Artists and left a number of fine pictorial records of 18th and early 19th century Dublin scenes. A memorial to Doctor William Ashford, the son of the artist, was erected by public subscription at Irishtown Green in 1894 as an appreciation of his medical services over half a century to the community.

In Victorian times Dan Lowrey, the king of Irish theatre impressarios and owner of the famous theatre in Dame Street (now the Olympia) resided at Sandymount Park. In this century it was renamed Roslyn Park and in 1947 a convent school was opened there but has recently closed. Austin Cooper, the antiquary, was a neighbour of Ashford at Sandymount in the early 1800s before he moved to another Gandon house, Abbeyville in Kinsealy, now the home of C.J. Haughey TD, the leader of Fianna Fáil. Burglars were very active in Sandymount in Cooper's time and in his letters he refers to having been robbed in October 1801 and August 1802, as was Ashford and several others.

In 1856 nuns of the Carmelite Order acquired a fine old house called Lakelands on Gilford Road and opened a convent and orphanage there. In 1870 Mother Mary Aikenhead, foundress of the Sisters of Mercy and her followers who had a nunnery on Sandymount Avenue since 1831, took over Lakelands. The Carmelites, in an exchange transaction, moved into Sandymount Avenue convent (now demolished), which was marked on 19th century maps as near Willfield.

Shortly after the arrival of the Sisters of Charity in Sandymount there was an outbreak of Asiatic Cholera which had a devastating effect throughout Dublin in 1832 and 1833. In 1833, under the supervision of their foundress, the sisters acquired a small store in Irishtown which was converted into a hospital for the cholera victims. A royal commission of inquiry was set up in 1833 into the condition of the poor in Ireland and Mother Mary Aikenhead gave a harrowing account to it of the sufferings of the poor, the destitute and the unemployed in this area.

Fairfield House, Newbridge Avenue, occupies the site of Haig's distillery, which was closed in 1833. In 1856 it was the hiding place of James Stephens, the founder and head centre of the Fenian Brotherhood. On November 11th that year the house was surrounded and Stephens was arrested along with other Fenian leaders, Charles Kickham, Hugh Brophy and Edward Duffy. Stephens

was not a prisoner for long however. On November 24th he escaped with the aid of prison staff who were Fenians.

J.B. Yeats, the father of another erstwhile Fenian, also lived in Sandymount for a time. Sandymount Castle was built on the village square by Richard Corbet, his brother-in-law. J.B. Yeats stayed at Sandymount Castle while a student in Trinity College. After his marriage to Susan P/ollexfen, Yeats moved into a newly built semi-detached house he called 'Georgeville' on Sandymount Avenue and it was here the poet William Butler Yeats was born on June 13th, 1865.

George Du Noyer, the geologist, artist and antiquarian, lived at 86 Seafort Avenue, Sandymount in the mid-1800s. He was a pupil of Petrie and was employed by the Ordnance Survey for which he did great work. Annie P. Smithson, the writer who helped nurse the wounded at Moran's Hotel during the Civil War, was born in Sandymount. The late Noel Purcell, the distinguished actor on stage and screen, lived for many years at 14 Sandymount Avenue.

During the mid-19th century several churches were built in the Sandymount area. St John's Anglican church on Park Avenue was the first to open in 1850 and was built mainly of granite with ornate facings of Caen stone from Normandy. The exterior facings of this beautiful church have deteriorated due to the wet climatic conditions here but the elaborate interior stonework remains intact.

St Mary's Star of the Sea Catholic church was the next to open, in 1853, and the Reverend John, Canon Hanlon, was parish priest here from 1880 to 1895. He is best remembered as the author of a history of the Irish saints. The Presbyterian church across the road from St Mary's Star of the Sea, was built about 1870, when the Rev Thomas Lyttle was first minister. The Presbyterians have now moved to the Methodist building at Sandymount Green, which was opened in 1864.

James Pearse, an English monumental sculptor lived with his family at three different addresses in the Sandymount area between 1886 and 1904. The first was No. 3 Newbridge Avenue, where he stayed 14 years until 1900, when he moved to No. 5 George's Villas, Sandy-

(Continued on Page 100)

SCALLED HILL OR SCALLET HILL (MODERN DAY SANDYMOUNT) WAS IN THE 13TH CENTURY THE PROPERTY OF RICHARD DE ST. OLOF, A CITIZEN OF DUBLIN. THE AREA WAS THEN DESCRIBED AS THE GREAT MEADOW BY THE SEA OR THE RABBIT WARREN.

SANDYMOUNT

JAMES STEPHENS

JOHN (CANON) O HANLON P.P.

IN THE EIGHTEENTH CENTURY SANDYMOUNT WAS KNOWN AS "BRICKFIELD TOWN" BECAUSE OF THE MANUFACTURE OF BRICKS THERE.

J WREN

W.B. YEATS

Santry

Sean Triabh

(The Old Tribe)

Santry of the old tribe (Sean Triabh) takes its name from some remote community of people in antiquity. According to the book of Lecan a sept called the Almanii inhabited this region of north Dublin in the distant past.

In the National Museum there are some flint artefacts which were found in the Santry area indicating that stone age man traversed these lands. In the 6th century Saint Pappin, the patron saint of the district, established a religious foundation here on the site of the present Protestant church. The townland of Poppintree near Ballymun is also associated with this holy man and is so named from the tree of Saint Pappin under which a patron was held in past centuries.

When the marauding Norse Vikings swept across the territory of Fingal in the 9th and 10th centuries Pappin's little monastic settlement at Santry, along will all the other churches and temples in north Dublin, were the objects of plunder and despoilation. As part of Fingal, Santry became the arena for the battle between the Viking invader and the native Gaels. In the 12th century this neighbourhood was plundered by Murcadh Ua Maeleachlainn, King of Meath, in revenge for the death of his son at the hands of Mac Gillamocholmog chief of Fingal.

With the coming of the Normans Hugh De Lacy, the Lord Palatinate of Meath, granted the lands of Santry to one of his barons, Adam De Phepoe, whose family retained these lands for many generations. The De Phepoes granted the church of Santry to the Abbey of St. Mary, in Dublin, which held it until the dissolution of the establishment in the 16th century.

In 1342 Francis De Phepoe of Santry was summoned by Edward III of England to join him with 15 men-at-arms and 25 halbardiers in the French wars. Thirty years later Johanna, the daughter of Francis De Phepoe, conveyed the lands of Santry to Thomas Mareward, who later became the Baron of Scryne.

In the 16th century the manor of Santry passed through marriage to the Nugent family and in 1581 William Nugent lost his estate here because of the part he took in the war against the English queen, Elizabeth. The Dublin merchant family of Barry next followed as proprietors of these lands and became the Lords of the manor of Santry. They erected the magnificent Queen Anne style mansion here in 1702.

Henry Barry, the 4th Baron Santry, was brought to trial before his peers in 1739 for the murder of a servant in a Palmerstown Inn. It is alleged that the young Lord Santry's life was saved by his uncle, Sir Compton Domville of Templeogue, who threatened to cut off the city water supply which passed through his land, if his nephew was not released. The young nobleman was however banished from Ireland and after some years of wandering about Europe, he died in Nottingham in 1751. His uncle Sir Compton Domville succeed him to the Santry estate. About 1800 the Domville line died out and the estate passed to their Scottish cousins, the Pocklingtons, who changed their name to Domville.

In December 1641 a detatchment of troops under the command of the governor of Dublin, the notorious Sir Charles Coote, advanced to Santry in the pursuit of Luke Netterville's insurgents. There the soldiers set upon some innocent Protestant and Catholic husbandmen in the local inn and butchered them without distinction

18th century newspapers referred to many incidents of highway robbery along the north coach road in the vicinity of Santry. In 1784 the church vestry here recommended to the parishioners to organise a public fund to reward those who apprehended and prosecuted all the robbers and thieves in the parish of Santry. In the following year the first parish constable was appointed. On 23rd May 1798 the Dublin Belfast mail coach was stopped and burned at the wall of Santry demesne by a party of insurgents. Later that evening five men suspected of being involved in the incident were captured by the patrolling attorneys corp. Local men, public house landlord big Jim Coughlane and Laurence Mooney, were whipped for participating in the attack, but their leader, the crippled Larry Clinch, made good his escape.

The Protestant church of St. Pappin was built in 1709 on the site of the mediaeval chapel which had become a roofless ruin. The lovely little village of Santry has all but disappeared, with the exception of one picturesque Swiss cottage which stands in Schoolhouse Lane. The Swiss village here dated to 1840 when Lady Domville on her return from a visit to Switzerland had the whole village reconstructed in the architectural style of that country. The large four storied red brick mansion of Santry Court, which was destroyed by fire in the 1940s, was once surrounded by vast pleasure grounds with well stocked fish ponds. 1958 saw the opening of the Morton Stadium on part of these grounds. On one memorable night in August of that year five world records were broken here.

OLD FORGE   SANTRY

SANTRY

SEAN TRIABH – OLD TRIBE

HENRY BARRY LAST LORD SANTRY

SANTRY COURT A MAGNIFICENT JACOBEAN MANSION WHICH WAS ERECTED IN 1702 WAS DESTROYED BY FIRE DURING THE NINETEEN FORTIES

IN MARCH 1798 THE MAIL COACH TO BELFAST WAS STOPPED AND THE PASSENGERS ROBBED AT SANTRY, AND IN MAY OF THAT YEAR THE COACH WAS BURNED BY A PARTY OF INSURGENTS AT THE WALL OF SANTRY DEMESNE.

Stoneybatter

P.W. Joyce in his 'Irish names of places' published in 1869 wrote that Bothar na gCloch or Stoneybatter was part of the great road which led from Tara to the Hurdle Ford at Dublin in Celtic times. This road was called the Slighe Cualann and was one of the five great highways constructed in second century Ireland in the Roman manner.

The name Bothar na gCloch or Stoneybatter undoubtedly indicated that it was of Celtic origin but it is not easy to prove the claim that it was part of the Slighe Cualann. Henry Morris in his paper 'The Slighe Cualann' (RSAJ Journal) June 1938 quoting from ancient MSS claims that this ancient highway passed through Kinsealy and Artane on to Dublin.

Early in the last century Rev. Nathaniel Burton published an interesting little book ('Oxmanstown and its environs') and recalled 18th century Stoneybatter as a "primitive place". Here there was a frieze market and Irish was spoken between its shopkeepers and their Co. Meath customers.

For centuries a maypole stood at Stoneybatter and Dubliners visited it annually to partake in the festivities of the Maypole. In 1773 it was cut down by the Authorities in consequence of a riot between soldiery from the Royal Barracks and the local populace. The newspaper of the day reported that the soldiers fired their muskets into the crowd and much damage was done to property, causing the suppression of another ancient Dublin custom. At that time there was a watch house at the end of Stoneybatter where the watch or police were stationed and there was also a pound.

Stoneybatter was a village on Oxmanstown Green where the Danes of Dublin settled after the Battle of Clontarf. Oxmanstown is a corruption of Oxmanstown or Eastmann town so called after the Danish invaders who came into Ireland from the East according to one source. In the 11th century Oxmanstown was famous for the fine oak wood and in 1098 King Rufus had oak imported from here to be used in the roof of Westminster Abbey.

Oxmanstown Green or Common was used for centuries as a place of assembly by Dubliners and it is recorded that a serious riot occurred there in 1495 and several citizens of rank were slain. Sporting contests took place there including hurling and football games long before the foundation of the GAA. John Wesley the founder of Methodism preached on Oxmanstown Green several times during his early visits to Ireland.

Oxmanstown Green once covered a wide area but today all that remains of it is an enclosed ground to the rere of the Incorporated Law Society's building at Blackhall Place. This building which was formerly the King's Hospital or Bluecoat school was built in 1773. It replaced an earlier school which stood at nearby Queen Street and was founded by Dublin Corporation and was granted a Royal Charter by Charles II in 1670. The Blackhall Place building was designed by Thomas Ivory and is a splendid example of Palladian architecture with its imposing facade and fine internal plasterwork.

Little John, Robin Hood's faithful lieutenant lived in the Oxmanstown area according to legend. The story goes that the giant outlaw fleeing the wrath of the Sheriff of Nottingham made his way to Dublin and became popular with the locals. Here he astonished all with his feats of archery but eventually was hanged at the Gibbets Slade, Arbour Hill.

Arbour Hill

A gallows stood on the summit of Arbour Hill for centuries and it is mentioned as early as 1192 in a riding to the Franchises report. This place was originally called Earbor or Arbhar (Irish) Hill meaning the hill of the corn for here were corn barns belonging to Christ Church cathedral in the middle ages.

The Gibbets Slade on Arbour Hill where Little John and Scaldbrother the robber met their end means the stream of the gallows. Before the Royal Barracks (Collins Barracks) was built in 1704 there was a public house at Arbour Hill called the Half Moon which was famous for its ale called apple d'or.

Wolfe Tone died in 1798 in the Provost prison, Arbour Hill which stands today in the grounds of Saint Bricins military hospital. Both Matthew Tone and Bartholomew Teeling were also imprisoned here and were executed at Arbour Hill. During the years 1866-67 the military prison at Arbour Hill held many soldiers who were arrested for involvement in the Fenian movement. Among these prisoners was John Boyle O'Reilly, a soldier in the Hussars who had recruited 80 members of his regiment to Fenianism before he was apprehended.

In this century Eamon de Valera and Brendan Behan were among those who saw the inside of Arbour Hill prison gates. In 1916 the bodies of the executed leaders were buried here in a quicklime grave where today the beautifully lettered memorial stands.

North Brunswick Street

North Brunswick St. which runs between Stoneybatter and Constitution Hill was originally called Channel Row and in the 17th century had two Benedictine convents. One of these convents stood at the rere of the present Richmond Hospital and was called King James's monastery after James II who opened it himself in 1689.

The Corporation opened a Workhouse in Nth. Brunswick St. in 1772 (now Morning Star Hostel) and thirty-one years later (1803) the Hardwick Fever Hospital was opened here. The Richmond Surgical Hospital followed in 1811 and the Whitworth Medical Hospital was built in 1817. These buildings were all designed by the great Irish architect Frances Johnston. The original Richmond Hospital building by Johnston was replaced in 1900 by a splendid redbrick ediface with copper domes and verandahs in the mock Elizabethan style.

The upper part of Stoneybatter became known as Manor Street in 1780 and was so called after Grangegorman Manor House. The tall red bricked building, No. 42 Manor St., a former police barracks, is said to have been the original Manor House but this is disputed. A village green once formed the junction of the present Aughrim-Prussia Streets when they were known as Blackhorse Lane and Cabra Lane respectively.

There is an entrance in Manor Street to the convent schools run by the Irish Sisters of Charity known as Stanhope Street school. Here Gorman the Dane gave his name to the district when he established his Grange farm on this site as a tenant of the Prior of the Church of the Holy Trinity (Christ Church). The Agard family lived here in Elizabethan times and later the Stanleys after whom nearby Stanley St. is named.

Much more could be written on this most interesting part of Dublin but one character which must be mentioned before we leave. He was known as "Billy the Bowl", having been born without legs he moved around in a large bowl fortified with iron. Although he was severely handicapped in this manner, Billy had very handsome features with dark cur-

(Continued on Page 100)

STONEYBATTER

An Bothar Clocach

Stoneybatter is an ancient street name which dates to the second century

FOR CENTURIES OXMANSTOWN GREEN WAS A VENUE FOR PUBLIC MEETINGS AND JOHN WESLEY PREACHED THERE SEVERAL TIMES.

THE GROUND TO THE RERE OF THE LAW SOCIETY HEADQUARTERS IN BLACKHALL PLACE IS ALL THAT REMAINS OF OXMANS-TOWN GREEN TO-DAY. HERE, IT IS SAID THAT LITTLE JOHN, ROBIN HOODS AID DE CAMP DEMONSTRATED FEATS OF ARCHERY.

JWREN

Swords

Sord   ## (The Pure Well)

Over the past two decades the rapid outward march of Dublin city has transformed the ancient village of Swords into a town of sizeable proportions. There was a settlement at Swords in the time of Alexander the Great for, according to the legend of the Milesian invasion, one of the companies of Heremon founded a fortress here called the high rath of Swords. This reference in the annals of the Four Masters to an early community here places Swords as older than Dublin city. From a 14th century manuscript Life of St. Columba we learn that St. Columcille dedicated a pure well (sord) after which the district was named and he is also said to have founded a church here.

The round tower adjoining the Church of Ireland building here marks the site of the ancient abbey of St. Columcille who, according to tradition, presented a missal written by himself to it and appointed St. Fionan Lobhar ("the leper") its first abbot. The establishment at Swords of a centre for the treatment of leprosy probably dates from the time of Fionan for during the early middle ages there was a leper hospital here at a place called Spittal Hill. A painting in the parish church (C. of I.) of a leper cured at the Pool of Bathseda recalls this fact.

The monastery at Swords grew in importance and wealth and became a target of the marauding Norsemen who sacked and plundered it on many occasions. It was burned at least six times between 1020 and 1166. A memorable event in the history of the monastery occured in 1014 when the bodies of Brian Boru and his son Murchad were carried here in solemn procession from the field of Clontarf. They remained overnight before the journey to Armagh for burial.

Beside the round tower stands the 14th century square belfry which is all that remains of the mediaeval prebendal church. The Church of Ireland edifice was completed in 1818 and was erected on the site of the mediaeval abbey which at that time had fallen into ruin.

About the year 1200 Swords became a Norman town of significance when the first Norman archbishop of Dublin, John Comyn built his manor house or palace here. Standing at the northern end of the town the ruins of the palace contain a chapel 17 feet wide by 50 feet long and a priest's or constable's room in a gateway tower. The archbishop's court was held here where the seneschal officiated in his Lordship's absence. Criminals were hanged on nearby Gallows Hill. In 1316 the Archiespicopal manor came under siege by the forces of Edward Bruce on their advance into Dublin. It was left in ruins and the Archbiship moved his residence to Tallaght.

In 1641 at a public meeting held at Swords, Luke Netterville of Corballis recruited a Fingallian armed force which he led in the rebellion of that year. After taking part in a number of engagements the little Fingallian army was finally cornered by crown forces at a place a mile to the south of Swords called the Bloody Hollow and were almost totally annihilated. Netterville however made good his escape.

Swords was known as a potwalloper borough from 1578 until the late 18th century because of the number of Protestant residents brought to live here by aspiring candidates for Parliament for the purpose of obtaining their votes. General Eyre Massey the veteran of Culloden and Quebec, who was M.P. for Swords in 1790, settled scores of veteran soldiers in the area.

A number of men of military character are associated with Swords. General Richard Montgomery of the American Revolutionary Army, who fell at the storming of Quebec, was born near here in 1736. Lte. Col. Molesworth Phillips, the explorer companion of Captain Cook, was born at Swords in 1755. A Cromwellian soldier named Hopkins who lived to 115 years of age was the sexton of Swords for many years and died there about 1745.

Swords was an ancient market town where for centuries people assemble around the old cross in the town centre to transact the business of buying the selling livestock and agricultural produce. King John granted to Archbishop Comyn the privilege of holding a fair for eight days after the feast of Columcille and this fair was incorporated by Elizabeth in 1578.

Over the centuries Swords was a haven for the weary traveller and was renowned for its inns and taverns. Sir William Brerton writing in 1635 found good accommodation at the Sign of the Boot and the other old inn names associated with Swords included The Harp, the Anchor, the Black Bull and the Royal Oak.

OLD BORO SCHOOLS SWORDS

SWORDS
SORD COLUMCILLE

AFTER THE BATTLE OF CLONTARF THE BODIES OF BRIAN BORU AND HIS SON MURROUGH WERE TAKEN TO THE MONASTERY OF SWORDS WHERE THEY WERE RESTED FOR A NIGHT BEFORE THEIR JOURNEY TO ARMAGH FOR BURIAL.

IT IS SAID THAT THE NAME SWORDS MEANS PURE FROM A WELL BLESSED BY COLUMCILLE WHEN HE FOUNDED A MONASTERY HERE ABOUT 560. A NINTH CENTURY ROUND TOWER AND A MEDIAEVAL BELFRY STANDS IN THE CHURCH OF IRELAND GROUND.

J.WREN '78

THE PICTURESQUE RUINS OF THE ARCHIEPISCOPAL PALACE OF SWORDS DATES BACK TO ABOUT 1200. THE ARCHBISHOPS OF DUBLIN LIVED HERE UNTIL 1327 WHEN THEY MOVED TO TALLAGHT.

Tallaght

Tamhleacht Muintir Parthalon
(The plague grave of the Parthalon)

This populous surburban development was until recent times a quiet village nestling at the foot of the Dublin hills. Tallaght takes its name from the gaelic "Tamhleact Muintir Parthalon", meaning the plague monument of the people of Parthalon, an ancient tribe who were wiped out by plague. It could be identified with an aboriginal bronze age population who left many tumuli and stone cairns scattered among the hills.

In the 8th century Saint Maelruan leader of the anchorite (Ceile De Culdee) reform movement founded the monastery of Tallaght which became one of the leading monastic settlements in Celtic Ireland. Oengus, one his disciples was author of the earliest Irish martyrology, the calendar of Oengus Cele De which was finished at Tallaght about the year 800.

St. Maelruan's monastery attracted students from all over Ireland and in the 9th century Tallaght and Finglas were known as the two eyes of Ireland. Beside the calendar of Oengus, two other ecclesiastical documents of great importance were written there, the martyrology of Tallaght in the 10th century and the celebrated Stowe missal in the 9th century.

Tallaght monastery suffered badly from Viking raids and in 811 they burned it to the ground. It was soon replaced by new buildings.

With the coming of the Anglo-Normans the monastic lands were transferred to the Norman Archbishops of Dublin, who built an archiepiscopal palace there which stood there until the 18th century. Archbishop Hoadley, the Protestant archbishop of Dublin in 1729 demolished the building. With the materials he built a new episcopal mansion which in turn, was taken down in 1825 by a Major Palmer the build a new mansion.

The warring Irish septs of the O'Tooles and O'Byrnes for hundreds of year descended from their mountain fastnesses upon the Anglo-Norman settlers at Tallaght plundering and laying waste to the countryside. In 1331 O'Toole of Imaal looted Tallaght and took away 300 sheep. When pursued by Sir Philip Brett a force of Dublin citizens he defeated them in a pitched battle.

The Dominicans came to Tallaght in 1842 and Major Palmer's fine house is incorporated in the Retreat House of the Priory.

St. Maelruan's Church of Ireland parish building (19th century) stands on the site of the original monastery and the later mediaeval parish church, with the mediaeval bell tower surviving. St. Maelruan's pattern was held at Tallaght for centuries on July 7th every year but, owing to excesses of drunkness and fighting, the pattern of "Moll Rooney" was supressed in 1874.

William Howard Russell, who was born at Jobstown, Tallaght, in 1820 gained fame as the first great war correspondent. Known as "Russell of the *Times*" his eye witness accounts of the horrors of the Crimean War and of the incompetence of the general staff led to public outcry and army reform.

On March 5th 1867 a Fenian rising was attempted at Tallaght. But Colonel Kelly, who commanded the insurgents, found that few of his men had guns. The majority had pikes and some were even unarmed. Standing no chance against the rifles of the well trained police when they confronted them at Tallaght police barracks, the Fenians were dispersed. The rising however was not a complete failure, for Fenians continued as a force in Irish affairs for the years that followed and their legacy influenced the rising of 1916.

A dam which held the water supply to the mediaeval city of Dublin was built at Balrothery near Tallaght in 1244. The course it took was through Templeogue, Kimmage, Mount Argus and Dolphins Barn to the city basin at James Street. Today the new satellite town of Tallaght to the south west of the city is comparable with Limerick in size. It has a population of over 60,000 people and is still expanding.

OLD BAWN HOUSE, ERECTED 1630
(NOW DEMOLISHED)

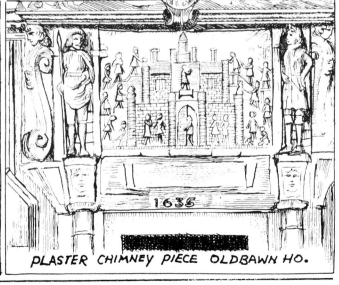

1635

PLASTER CHIMNEY PIECE OLDBAWN HO.

TALLAGHT
(TAIMHLEACHT)
A PLAGUE MONUMENT

ACCORDING TO BARDIC TRADITION 9000 PEOPLE OF THE ANCIENT TRIBE OF PARTHALON PERISHED BY PLAGUE AND WERE BURIED AMONG THE TALLAGHT HILLS.

THE MONASTERY FOUNDED BY ST. MAELRUAN AT TALLAGHT IN THE 8TH CENTURY WAS ONE OF THE MOST IMPORTANT IN THE EARLY CELTIC CHURCH.

IN 1867 A FENIAN RISING WAS ATTEMPTED AT TALLAGHT BUT THE ILL-EQUIPPED INSURGENTS HAD FEW GUNS, THEY MOSTLY CARRIED PIKES AND WERE DISPERSED BY A WELL ARMED CONSTABULARY

S. WREN '78

Lucan

(Continued from Page 62)

Swift. In one couplet he refers to:
'Agmondisham Vesey, out of great bounty,
Built the bridge at the expense of the county'
In fact Vesey built the old bridge at Lucan at his own expense.

About the same time as Lucan House was built, the Speaker of the Irish House of Commons, the Right Honourable Edmund Sexton Perry, built St Edmondsbury nearby. The Viceroy was entertained there in 1783. Pery was later made Viscount Pery but this did not stop him from opposing the Act of Union in 1800, although he moved to London afterwards and died there in 1806.

It was during the late eighteenth century that Lucan acquired its reputation as a spa. The sulphurous spring was discovered in 1758 and became a centre for polite society and fashionable invalids. The bottled spring water could also be purchased in Dublin. Besides the spa, employment was provided by a cotton mill and iron works in the village.

At the end of the century the great architect James Gandon came to live at Lucan. He was the creator of many of Dublin's finest buildings, including his masterpiece the Custom House. He died at his home in Canonbrook, Lucan, in 1823.

John Collins, one of the leading Irish tenors of the 19th century, was born and bred in Lucan. He was discovered in the summer of 1829 working as a cook in the kitchens of his father's establishment, the Spa Hotel. He was only 19 when he was overheard by a visiting operatic company dining at the hotel after performing at the Theatre Royal.

He made his London debut in the Haymarket on August 29th, 1832, as Captain MacHeath in the 'Beggar's Opera'. He was soon engaged as the principal singer with the Haymarket company. He made his first Dublin appearance in the Theatre Royal in February 1833, when the top Irish comedian of the day, Tyrone Power, was also appearing there. In 1835 Collins was given star billing as a lyric artist at Covent Garden, when he played the part of a highwayman in Fitzball's burletta of 'Paul Clifford', in which a real coach and six horses were used on the stage.

In 1846 he went to America, where he first appeared at the Park Theatre, New York. He became a special favourite at the Old Broadway Theatre in New York and spent most of the remainder of his career in America. In 1864 he commenced a European tour and, in April 1865, he returned to the Theatre Royal after an absence of 10 years. He appeared as Sir Patrick Plenipo and Rory O'Moore and received a rousing welcome on this, his last visit to his native land. In 1866 he toured Australia and then returned to the United States, where he died in Philadelphia on August 13th, 1873.

During the nineteenth century Lucan went into decline. The local cotton mill closed, the spa became less fashionable and the main road to the west was diverted around the village. By the early twentieth century local industry was largely based on serving the surrounding agricultural community. By 1913, when the ITGWU launched its farm labourers section one of the first new branches were formed in Lucan. A strike called at harvest time saw wages raised from 14 shillings a week (70p) to 17 shillings (85p). Workers in the local flour mills owned by W E Shackleton, a prominent Sinn Féin member, were locked out in the same year for joining the ITGWU. Some farmers also evicted labourers from their cottages for refusing to leave the union during the great lock out of that year. When the Irish Citizen Army was established to protect strikers in confrontations with the police a company was formed in Lucan.

Killester

(Continued from Page 60)

by nuns from the great north county Dublin monastery of Grace Dieu after its dissolution in the 16th century by Henvy VIII. A tree lined path called the Nuns' Walk, a section of which still survives at the entrance to Killester United Soccer Club, may have been connected to the convent.

The manor house built by the Cootes at Killester was destroyed by fire in 1919. Afterwards some of the fittings, including a venetian window and chimney piece were installed at Howth Castle by Lutyens, the architect.

Furry Park House, which stands behind O'Reilly's garage on the Howth Road at Killester is one of the oldest houses in north Dublin still occupied. It was built in 1730 by Joseph Fade, a Dublin merchant banker. Among the many residents at Furry Park House were Richard Boyle, Earl of Shannon, Judge T. V. Vandeleur, Charles Kendal, Bushe, who was Lord Chief Justice of Ireland from 1822 to 1841, Sir Ralph Cusack, chairman of the Midland and Great Western Railway and Mrs. Moya Llewellyn Davies, a friend of W. B. Yeats and Michael Collins, frequent visitors to the House. An assassination attempt on Collins was made there during a visit in the Civil War and those involved are reputed to have been taken down to Clontarf and executed on the spot by Collins's bodyguards.

This well preserved building which has been under threat of demolition came under a High Court restoration judgement in 1986.

Dun-Laoghaire

(Continued from Page 48)

and the house itself became a school before being demolished.

Echo Lodge dates back to the same period. It still stands as the centrepiece of the Dominican convent off Lower George's Street. The Dominicans bought it in 1847 and added two large wings.

Fairyland, at the top of York Road, also dates from the early 1800s. It probably

owes its survival to acquisition by the Christian Brothers. Adjoining it were two old farmhouses, Airhill and Racefield. Racefield took its name from the old Dun Laoghaire race course, which occupied the present site of the town golf course.

The 1830s saw the growth of terraced housing throughout the area and the construction of various mansions on Tivoli Road, including Primrose Hill – the home of Alexander Findlater, who built Findlater's church in Dublin.

By far the most impressive of the new buildings were Granite Hall and Stoneview. Both were constructed by George Smyth, the stone contractor for the harbour, and were built of Dalkey granite. Granite Hall was demolished in the 1950s but Stoneview still survives, albeit in a dilapidated condition.

(Continued from Page 64)

Malahide

working hours. The very first of these mills in Ireland was built by the Norsemen of Dublin in 836.

Yellow Walls, the area of Malahide south of the estuary, was also a scene of early industry. It first appears on a map of 1756 as a small hamlet between Peas Fields Hill and Gay Brook Stream. It acquired its name from the yellow stains left by vegetable stains used on silks, woollens and linen manufactured locally.

One of the oldest and most distinctive buildings in Malahide is Robswalls Castle to which a Victorian house is now attached. It stands on the main road between Malahide and Portmarnock. In the early middle ages the Cistercian monks of St Mary's Abbey in Dublin leased and controlled the castles guarding Dalkey and Malahide harbours. All fishermen using Malahide harbour had to pay a seasonal rent of 600 fish to them at Robswell. The origin of the name is uncertain and it has been variously called Roebuck's Wall and Robertswall castle too. Paddy's hill, which legend has it marks the spot where St Patrick first received a welcome in Ireland after being driven away by natives from the Wicklow coast, is behind it. The owners of the castle – and it tended to pass back and forth between the Talbots and the Barnewells, another old Fingal family – were entitled to claim all flotsam and jetsam washed ashore from wrecks on this part of the coast and are rumoured to have had a highly profitable trade before the coast guard was set up in 1830.

During the 18th and 19th centuries Malahide was a major fishing port. Cod, shellfish and prawns were the main catch. The Malahide yawls were "the admiration of all" who visited harbours along the east coast according to one observer in 1863. Their main fishing areas were the Irish Sea between Arklow and the Isle of Man. On November 14th, 1828 a yawl with four fishermen on board capsized in the harbour and only one body, that of Michael Gaffney, was recovered for burial in Malahide Abbey. The building of the Dublin-Drogheda railway viaduct in 1844, cutting off the estuary from the sea seriously affected the fishing industry which had become extinct by this century.

The railway viaduct was built by Robert McEntire, a local silk merchant who owned a silk mill and ribbon factory at Killeen Terrace. He built a fine house on the site for his only daughter as a marriage present. She decided to take Holy Orders instead and entered a convent in Drumfries, where she eventually became abbess. But even today the building is known as the Dowry House.

Another prominent building in Malahide is the Grand Hotel built in 1835 by James Fagan. During the recent state visit of. US president Ronald Reagan it played host to the combined crews of US Airforce One and Two, the president's personal aircraft. It regularly hosts major meetings in its new conference centre. At the opposite end of the village is the famous fishmongers, M Wright and Sons, whose premises are the old RIC barracks destroyed by the IRA in the 1920s.

The famous nationalist family of the Kettles lived nearby in Drinam House, where a major new housing estate is being built today across the former greenbelt between Malahide and Swords. Andrew Kettle farmed the land as a tenant of the Russell-Cruises, prominent Catholic landlords. Later he lived at Millview in Malahide. He was a great natural athlete and according to local legend was the only man who could not only lift the blacksmith's anvil at Kinsealy but throw it over his head and out the door. He is best known as a staunch supporter of Parnell and the Land League. His son Tom was an MP and member of the Irish Parliamentary Party, as well as a considerable poet. He answered Redmond's call to fight for the right of small nations in the first World War and was killed at the battle of the Somme in September 1916. His father Andrew died a few days after receiving the news on September 22nd.

(Continued from Page 88)

Sandymount

mount Avenue, and from 1901 to 1904 he resided at No. 1 Lisreaghan Terrace, Sandymount Avenue. James Pearse was in fact the father of Patrick and Willie Pearse, who were executed after the 1916 Rising. The Pearse brothers spent all their boyhood and student days in Sandymount and Patrick was present in 1904 when Gaelic League branches were formed there and in Ringsend. In 1914, after the formation of the Irish Volunteers, there were assemblies and drill practices held on Sandymount Green.

Two or three years after the foundation of the Gaelic Athletic Association there were three Gaelic football teams playing in the Sandymount-Ringsend area, The Fontenoys, Isle of the Sea and Sons of the Sea. The most famous of these clubs, Isles of the Sea, won three Dublin county championships with all local born players and also the All-Ireland football final in 1901. The Fontenoys club, which is still in existence, was also wellknown for its hurlers and won its first junior hurling title in 1904. In 1968 it amalgamated with Clanna Gael. The Shelbourne soccer club had a ground near Sandymount Catholic church in 1918, which had earlier been opened as the headquarters of the Sandymount Cricket and Bowling Club in 1870.

On July 20th 1864, Sandymount Cricket Club hit up the huge total of 524 against Co. Wicklow, at Sandymount. It was the highest score made in Irish cricket up to that time. Sandymount were keener on batting records that day, than on winning the match. They batted from

12 noon until 5.30, leaving Wicklow just half-an-hour to bat!

James Gilligan hammered the bowling for 200 and was the first man to reach that mark in Irish cricket. R. Snow went in at No. 7 and hit 103. J. Doran, R. St. Leger, L. Flanagan and F. McKenna also piled on the runs, and the Extras chipped in 47, with 32 wides.

Charles Stewart Parnell was playing for Wicklow, and he took three wickets. The bowling figures wre not given in the "Irish Times" report, and that could have been some slight relief for the Wicklow bowlers. Many stories have been told about Parnell's captaincy of Co. Wicklow. These stories, which may have gained in the telling, suggest he was an autocrat. Certainly, after playing in that match at Sandymount he was never likely to give much to opponents!

Wicklow, in their 30 minutes batting scored five runs and lost 3 wickets, all to Gilligan. So after all the fireworks and records, they were not beaten.

(Continued from Page 70)

Portmarnock

(Continued from Page 92)

Stoneybatter

Dubliner and his wife, Mary Elizabeth de Pree, a widow, was a member of the famous Haig whiskey family in Scotland. Tradition has it that this led Jameson to establish his own famous distilling company. His wife died in 1918 and John Jameson two years afterwards. Both are buried in the local cemetery beside the ruins of St Marnock's, which was also the name they gave their own home. Guglielmo Marconi, the pioneer of radio and telegraphy, was a nephew of the Jamesons and frequently visited St Marnock's.

Portmarnock House, the centuries old home of the Plunketts, which contained beautiful stained glass windows in the west wing, was destroyed by fire in 1953. The area was also the site of the famous Portmarnock brickworks which was operated by the Plunketts for over 200 years. The red and yellow bricks manu-

factured there can still be seen in the buildings of Georgian and Victorian Dublin.

Francis Elrington Ball, the historian and author of 'The History of County Dublin' was born at Portmarnock and the brilliant Victorian artist Walter Osborne spent the summer months in a cottage here for a number of years and painted the picturesque coastline.

ling hair and was a great favourite among the fair sex. For a number of years he was seen begging around the Stoneybatter area where he was well supported. About this time there was some unsolved murders in the countryside around here and some citizens suspected Billy of these foul crimes although they could not prove anything.

Eventually his career of crime came to an end when he failed in an attempt to rob two unsuspecting ladies while they were walking through the fields of Arbour Hill. He engaged the ladies in conversation and suddenly with the herculean strength of his powerful arms dragged them down with the intention of relieving them of their valuables. In the struggle however, one lady managed to prod his eye with her thumb and leaving him in agony while they made their escape. "Billy the Bowl" spent the remainder of his days in Green Street jail where he became an object of great curiosity.

Index

Acknowledgements to Ms Patricia Seager, Assistant Director, Dublin Millennium, for kind assistance and permission to use Millennium logo.